the smart divorce®

SMART GUIDES

save time, money – and your sanity

DEBORAH MOSKOVITCH

THE SMART DIVORCE PUBLICATIONS

The information contained in the Smart Guides is general in nature and does not constitute authoritative legal advice or psychological counsel. Laws vary according to state or jurisdiction and may have been amended since publication. This smart guide should be used only in consultation with a licensed lawyer who is properly familiar with the specific legal matter in question. To acquire specific legal advice you need to seek the counsel of a qualified family law lawyer. To acquire psychological counsel, you will want to consult with a qualified psychological specialist.

The Smart Divorce® is a registered trademark of Deborah Moskovitch and The Smart Divorce. This book or any portion thereof is copyrighted, and may not be distributed, modified, or reproduced, or used in any manner whatsoever without advance permission in writing from the publisher, Deborah Moskovitch.

If you have questions about using any of our copyrighted materials, please write your detailed request to Deborah Moskovitch.

For more information visit www.thesmartdivorce.com
and you may contact Deborah by email at info@thesmartdivorce.com
or by calling 905.695.0270

The Smart Divorce Smart Guides

Copyright © 2014 Deborah Moskovitch

First Printing 2012

ISBN 978-0-9880893-4-1

The Smart Divorce Publications

Cover and Interior Design: Deborah Moskovitch (cover) and Sarah Battersby

The Smart Guides

1. Planning for a Smart Divorce
2. Coping with the Stress of the Emotional Divorce
3. How to Increase Your Ability to Cope When Divorcing
4. A Journey Toward Forgiveness Following Divorce
5. Legal Separation - The Power of Setting Realistic Expectations
6. Understanding Your Divorce Options
7. Finding a Good Divorce Lawyer
8. Understanding How Assets Get Divided in Divorce
9. Getting Your Finances and Record Keeping Organized for Divorce
10. Financial Information Checklist
11. Important Financial Steps Required to Prepare for Divorce
12. How to Tell Your Children You're Divorcing
13. Smart Co-Parenting and Putting Your Children's Best Interest First
14. Cooperative Parenting or Parallel Parenting
15. Living Separate and Apart
16. Smart Co-Parenting for the New Family Unit
17. How to Tell Your Spouse You Want a Divorce
18. What to Tell the Kids About a High-Conflict Co-Parent
19. A B.I.F.F. Response to Hostile Email
20. Separating Safely: Knowing the Risks of Abuse
21. Domestic Violence: Is it Time to Leave?
22. Divorcing with Post Traumatic Stress: Getting the Help You Need
23. Separating Safely: Are You Abusive?

The Smart Divorce Team

	Name	Phone	Address
Family members			
Lawyer			
Therapist			
Accountant			
Financial Planner			
Mediator			
Arbitrator			
Parenting Expert			
Children's Therapist			
Massage Therapist			
Babysitter			
Friends			
Support Groups			
Clergy			
Gym			
Other			

Planning For A Smart Divorce

Divorce is an extremely challenging time in your life. But it does not have to be a legal, financial or emotional nightmare. When you are well informed and prepared for what you need to do to navigate the process and practicalities of divorce, you can have a much smoother transition while keeping your family, finances and sanity intact.

The Smart Divorce® provides you with the tools and techniques that will allow you to stay on a smart and measured track throughout the divorce process. Both a process and a step by step program, The Smart Divorce helps you to strategize and to be smart about divorce, to overcome conflicts, fears and obstacles, and to move forward in your life with focus, hope and confidence.

What is a Smart Divorce?

Divorce rarely goes through without a hitch — especially when children, properties and finances are involved. Emotional turmoil and everyday chaos almost always accompany the early stages of divorce. However, it is at this time that legal issues come up and you are faced with a myriad of decisions when you are least prepared to deal with them objectively.

With a smart divorce, however, you are able to manage the

> Keep the "two divorces" — the emotional divorce and the legal divorce — as separate as possible.

competing legal and emotional sides of divorce to ensure you make the best possible decisions for you and your family, as well as minimize your conflicts and costs. You learn how to keep the "two divorces" — the emotional divorce and the legal divorce — as separate as possible. You will be able to understand your emotions and deal with them with the help of a therapist and friends. This, in turn, will help you to be in the proper frame of mind to treat your legal divorce as a business transaction, and as a job you basically have to do to put your children's best interests first, to arrive at a successful settlement, to move on to a better life for you and your spouse.

The smart approach to divorce:

- affirms the emotions experienced in marital breakups
- helps you process your legal options and lawyers early on
- assists you in making informed decisions, protected from the damage that uncontrolled emotions can cause
- provides you with questions to help guide your decision making when assessing the right legal fit
- guides you in putting your children's best interests first
- moves you and your spouse back into single status, ready to get on with the rest of your lives while fulfilling the responsibilities that flow from your former married state

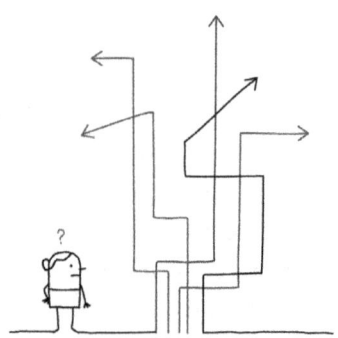

Why is it critical that you get a smart divorce? Because you — and your children, if you have any, — are going to be living the rest of your lives with the results of the decisions you make during your divorce process. You want to make decisions that will allow all of you to live without regret.

How The Smart Guides Will Help You Be **SMART** about your divorce:

Start with realistic goals and objectives.

Maximize your knowledge and information.

Avoid being emotionally reactive.

Retain the best divorce team you can afford.

Treat your divorce as a business transaction.

Your divorce is a journey. The Smart Guides help you to navigate and to break down in steps what you need to do to get through the process and practicalities of divorce as well as to accomplish specific objectives:

- Manage the emotional divorce and develop a support network
- Understand the divorce options and resolutions available to you
- Interview and choose the right divorce lawyer
- Assess if your lawyer is a good fit
- Know how to prepare and bring the right financial information to your lawyer
- Consider your children's best interests
- How to make smart decisions so that you can move forward with focus, hope and confidence.

The Smart Divorce Resource ToolKit is designed to meet your needs – to save you time, money and your sanity. Divorce can be rich in opportunity to learn and grow from. Effectively managing the divorce process will lead you to a greater understanding of what needs to be done in the best interests of your family and yourself.

2

Coping with the Stress of the Emotional Divorce

Divorce has become so common that people underestimate how powerful an experience it truly is. When someone that we love dies, most of us accept that we need to mourn, to reach out for love and support, and to take good care of ourselves. To heal from divorce, it is just as essential to grieve, to work through the pain, and to adopt good coping skills.

If at times you feel emotionally and physically fragile, you are not alone: divorce is stressful. In fact, on a classic rating scale of stressful life events, divorce consistently ranks second only to the death of a spouse or child. Instead of trying to simply soldier on, it is vital for you to recognize that stress can take its toll on your emotional and physical health, and result in fatigue, anxiety, sleep disruption, depression, headaches, back problems, and other potentially serious health issues.

The important thing to know is that you can and will get through the stress and distress of divorce. These positive coping skills will help you to protect your health and to feel stronger and better too.

Maintain Good Physical Health

Attention to good health habits is like insurance: protect yourself now to help protect your health later.

Increase your exercise. Regular exercise helps keep you physically fit and does wonders for relieving anxiety, tension and anger. If you need extra motivation to stick with a routine, join a gym, take a class, or work out with a trainer or a friend.

Maintain a healthy diet. Try not to skip any meals, to eat healthy and wholesome foods and to stay hydrated. Good food is fuel for your body and mind.

Get good sleep. Take a bath, read a book or relax before bed. Keep your bedroom dark and at a cooler temperature to promote sleep. See your doctor if you are having sleep difficulties.

Eliminate harmful habits. Avoid smoking, drinking and other potentially destructive coping habits. This will help you to maintain the energy, focus and concentration to make good decisions.

Take care of your emotional needs. By nurturing your emotional health, you will also protect your physical wellbeing. Now is a good time to talk to a therapist or counsellor to take care of both your own and your children's emotions.

Recognize the difference between stress and depression. Feeling sad and anxious during divorce is normal. But if you find that you have low energy, difficulty motivating yourself, too much or too little appetite, trouble falling or staying asleep, or thoughts of running away or even hurting yourself, you may be suffering from depression. Talk to your family doctor and seek help from a qualified therapist so that you can feel better again.

Nurture Your Emotional Health

Surrounding yourself with helpful professionals, finding ways to feel and work through your emotions are important and healthy strategies for reducing your stress. There are many resources you can put in place to help you. People deal with changes in their lives in different ways. Some like to work it out on their own and others want to talk it out with a professional. If you ignore the grieving, somewhere, later on, it will catch up to you and may cause you difficulty with moving forward.

Speak with a neutral third party. A therapist will help you to confront your fears and what you can do to overcome them. You will be able to safely explore what happened in your marriage and how it unraveled. This insight into your marriage and other issues will help you to cope with your grief, take ownership for what went wrong, and understand your own vulnerabilities so that you don't repeat patterns in new relationships. To find a therapist, ask your family doctor, lawyer or friends who have been helped for a referral. Or contact your local psychological association your company's Employee Assistance Program.

Share with someone you respect. A member of the clergy, or someone other than a friend who you hold in high regard might be an impartial third party you can talk to.

Join a support group. You can get support and learn from others who have had a similar life experience, as well as possibly make some new friends who truly understand what you are going through.

Make time for family and friends. The people who love you can often be your cheerleaders and will help to look out for you.

More Strategies to Cope with Stress

Reframe your thinking: managing your divorce is a process, not a crisis.

It is better to manage your emotions than to be managed by emotional baggage. The emotions you are feeling — whether positive or negative — are normal. Whether you are sad, angry or hurt, it is important to explore and work through your emotions with a safe person such as a therapist or counsellor. Gradually the emotional weight will lift and allow you to gain control.

Take control and manage your finances. This will empower and give you a sense of control over what is happening with your budget: how much comes in and what goes out each month, where you can increase your savings, how to plan for your budget and financial needs.

You can't go through life feeling like a victim or someone who needs to be rescued. If you want a fulfilling life, start doing small things to achieve your long terms goals. Making a little effort to meet new people and enjoy new pursuits will help you to build a positive post-divorce outlook.

> Realize that some people feel uncomfortable with divorce —- but this is their problem, not yours.

Be introspective. There are few rituals around divorce and people can say hurtful things. Realize that some people feel uncomfortable with divorce —- but this is their problem, not yours.

Put your children's best interests first. This is your priority. Tell your children that you love them and that the divorce is not their fault. This will give them a sense of security.

Divorce is a problem to be solved, not a war to be won. By recognizing your divorce-related stress, facing your feelings, and putting effective coping skills and habits in place, you will be able to move forward with focus, hope and confidence.

How to Increase Your Ability to Cope When Divorcing

"In theory there is no difference between theory and practice. In practice there is."
~Yogi Berra

It is somewhat misguided to subscribe to the theory that divorce sits in a certain position, or carries a certain weight, on a scale of stressful life events. If that were the case, then all those who go through a divorce would experience exactly the same amount of stress; and the individual would be unable to manage better on some days than others. Any "helping" person who deals with divorcing couples can testify to the fact that, different divorcing persons respond differently to their situation; and as individuals are able to manage it better on some days than on others. So if it isn't the phenomenon of divorce that is the major source of stress, then what is? The great poet John Milton gave us a clue when he said, "... the mind is its own place, and in itself can make a Heaven of Hell, a Hell of Heaven".

Of course divorce can be stressful, but it does not carry a consistent weight for all, we can magnify our response by the way we interpret our situation. Those who think logically and create realistic expectations, in relation to the divorce, will manage better than those who hold unrealistic beliefs and expectations. This Smart Guide is designed to help you minimize the demands of the divorce process. In order to manage well these demands that are being placed upon you, during the course of the divorce, it is preferred that you are in control of your own head; and no one else.

Coping Mantras

In the Buddhist tradition a mantra is regarded as a "guard"; a guard against illusion taking over the mind. I have written these "tips" in the form of mantras. They are concise and easy to remember. Different ones will be meaningful to you at different times during the process. When you need to, you can repeat it (silently) to yourself. The more you repeat it, the less you will have to remind yourself; it will become second nature.

What is, is.

This is the first of two universal laws. There is no use fretting about what could have been or should have been. As an ancient Greek philosopher once said, "everything is exactly as it should be". In the case of a fatal motor vehicle accident, there will be many who cluck their tongues and say, "what a tragedy, that should never have happened". However, what do you suppose is going to happen when you combine excessive speed, alcohol, a ton of metal, and a slippery road surface? Considering all the elements throughout the history of your relationship, and laying blame on no one, divorce is exactly what should be happening. You may not like it, or wish it was otherwise, but to tell yourself that it shouldn't be happening is like chasing a mirage; and as mirages cannot be caught, the chase can become exhausting.

One thing follows another.

This is the second of the two universal laws. You will not be happy until you are finished with whatever painful emotion you are creating in the present; and that misery is a direct result of whatever you are saying to yourself about your situation. If, for example, you are consumed with anger, you will not be happy until you are done with the anger; and that means thinking logically about the object of your anger. The most common thinking error in these situations is called "absolute thinking" and is loaded with what's right, wrong, fair, unfair, equitable, and inequitable about others' behaviour; or what they should or should not be doing. Hundreds of years ago Aristotle gave us the logic when he said, "People always do what they should be doing" (for themselves!). You may disagree with the behaviour, but if you tell yourself it shouldn't be happening you are chasing another mirage. People do what they do "for" themselves not "to" you!

> It is much more logical to ask yourself, "what are the realistic odds that what I fear will occur?"

One hole (step) at a time.

The golfers in the crowd will recognize this one. Golf is a game best played one hole at a time. If you are regretting something you did on the last hole, or anticipating the challenge of the next hole you're going to blow the one you are on. Life is the same thing; it is best played one hole (step) at a time. There is nothing you can do about the past; it is gone. You cannot change it. You can only learn from it. If you don't want to feel like this again, don't make the same mistake! Likewise, there is nothing you can do about the future; it isn't here yet. When you catastrophize (i.e. "what if . . . ") you have jumped into the future and are trying to convince yourself that you are a fortune teller. It is much more logical to ask yourself, "what are the realistic odds that what I fear will occur?" The chances are rarely worse than fifty-fifty; and if that's the case, why focus on the negative fifty? You are only able to be effective in the present, you have no power over past or future.

Can I be sure?

There is a great temptation during a conflict to convince yourself that you are a "mind reader". It is not uncommon during periods of heightened emotion to assert that you know that another party thinks in a particular manner about some topic. Based upon the degree to which you know the other party, there may be a probability that you know, but there is no one hundred percent certainty that you do. People can change their minds about things, especially when they receive new information. You might have increased certainty about what someone believes if the belief was asserted in your presence; but even then it could have been stated under duress and/or subject to change later. If you accept one of your hypotheses as fact you could end up like the star of this story:

> There was once a traveller who got a flat tire, late at night, in a remote rural area. He pulled over to the side of the road and looked about for some sign of life. He spotted a farmhouse, with the porch light on, several hundred metres down the road. He began to walk toward the light, but as he walked he began to imagine what the farmer might say. The traveller imagined that the farmer would be hesitant to open the door so late at night, let alone loan him a wrench to change his tire. As he approached the farmhouse the traveller had played out his unsuccessful attempts to influence the farmer several times in his imagination. In the traveller's mind the farmer could not be convinced to trust him. As he opened the door the farmer asked, "how can I help you?" with a friendly smile on his face.
>
> The traveller mindlessly blurted out, "you can keep your damn wrench!!"

Whenever you catch yourself in the act of reading someone's mind ask yourself, "can I be sure?"

.366; one of life's greatest secrets

The best lifetime batting average belongs to Ty Cobb. He was the most successful hitter that major league baseball has ever seen and he failed to hit the ball more than six times out of ten. His lifetime batting average was .366. Learn to live with your mistakes. Don't confuse yourself with your mistakes; there is a difference. You are not your mistakes. If you don't like the way you feel as a result of a mistake you made don't make it again! Learn from your mistakes. Evolve. Adapt. There is no need for you to be perfect. Getting a hit three and a half times out of ten will get you into the Hall of Fame.

> There is no use fretting about what could have been or should have been.

Manage Your Expectations

Holding unrealistic goals for yourself and others will only set you up for failure, and the resultant misery. Choose your battlefields, you can't win them all. An ancient Asian military strategist once said, that the best commander was not the one who had one hundred triumphs in one hundred battles but the one who used strategy to defeat one hundred opponents without ever stepping on the battlefield. Manage your own expectations. Be practical. Hold realistic expectations of others. Set realistic goals. Advance in stages. Of course aspirations are important! But never forget, you will only reach what you aspire to, one step at a time. Ask anyone who has topped Mt. Everest!

Be a Mountain

Nothing can move you; neither good nor bad! You understand that these are relative concepts. What you initially view as good (and allow yourself to become overly pleased, proud, cocky, or confident about) can soon become bad (and now you crash!). On the other hand, what you initially interpret as bad (and allow yourself to become totally "bummed out" over) can soon become good. All parts of the continent are the same; when the sun is shining, the clouds are right around the corner, and when it's raining the sun is never far away. On September 11, 2001, there were a bunch of people in the Logan and Dulles airports who were some angry about missing their flights to New York city, until . . .

> Manage your own expectations. Be practical. Hold realistic expectations of others.

> There were no "bad guys" involved in the demise of the relationship, not you, or the other party. You were each acting like human beings and attempting to get your needs met.

Take the High Road

I'm sure you would like to enter the next chapter of your life with an absence of baggage left over from your present relationship. The more oppositional, antagonistic, or combative you become, during the divorce process, the more likely it is that you will contribute to the creation of "unfinished business" that you will carry with you into the next chapter. Human behaviour is determined interactionally. You and the other party are locked in a "dance" whereby you are each being influenced by the other, and influencing the other all at the same time. All that to say, that people will reciprocate "heavy tactics". No one likes to come to agreement under threat or coercion. We all would like the freedom to choose.

You can increase your ability to "take the high road" by looking at your relationship logically. There were no "bad guys" involved in the demise of the relationship, not you, or the other party. You were each acting like human beings and attempting to get your needs met. Unfortunately, the two of you created a dissatisfying interaction in your efforts to do so. The fault lies in the interaction, not in the parties.

Cope Don't Mope

Human beings are reward burning machines. We need reward (reinforcement) in order to maintain self esteem, confidence, energy and the like. We get our reward from a variety of sources including friends, work, and recreation. We have a tendency, during difficult times, to pull back from our sources of reward, enter into isolation, and begin to mope. Just at the time when we need reinforcement the most, we have the least. Do not abandon your sources of reward! You will not feel good first and then want to be with friends, go to the gym, go to work, work on your hobby, or take a course. Feeling good comes from being with your friends, working out regularly, working, getting into your hobby, or finally taking that course you've always wanted to. Feeling good comes from coping, not before it.

Be Prepared To Change

Those organisms in nature that meet with the most success are those that can adapt to change. Those organisms that are rigid and inflexible will surely perish; do you remember the dinosaurs? Having the willingness and the ability to change is not an admission of some flaw of yours that needs to be addressed, but of your intelligence. Your willingness is the recognition of a challenge that sometimes requires transformational change.

Here's another little story to help you with your transformation:

> There was once a little stream that wandered across the country, easily finding its way around rocks and through mountains. Then it came to a desert. The stream tried to cross the desert using the same methods it used with other barriers it had encountered. The old methods didn't work. When the stream ran into the sand, it disappeared; it lost its identity. It tried and it tried but to no avail. The stream asked, "Could this be the end, is there no way for me to continue?"
>
> Then a voice came out of the wind and said, "If you stay the way you are you will not cross the sand, you must lose yourself to find yourself again". The stream responded, "But if I lose myself, I will never know what I am supposed to be." "On the contrary", said the voice, "if you lose yourself you will become more than you ever dreamed you could be".
>
> So the little stream decided to surrender itself to the sun and it evaporated into the heavens, transformed into clouds . . . a sort of death. The clouds were carried many kilometers across the great desert. Then the little stream poured from the clouds as a cleansing rain upon the earth and formed a new stream that continued on its journey.

Information and guidance provided by Mike Webster, Ed.D., R.Psych
You may contact Dr. Webster by e-mail at conman@uniserve.com

Dr. Mike Webster is a Registered Psychologist specializing in conflict management. He is a marital therapist that has worked in the police universe for over 30 years. He also advises law enforcement agencies, both domestically and internationally on the management of hostage/barricade incidents, kidnappings, incidents of public disorder and crisis intervention.

A Journey Toward Forgiveness Following Divorce

Have you been deeply wounded by your ex-spouse? Does s/he continue to engage in hurtful behavior even though you are no longer living under the same roof? Are you finding it difficult to move beyond feelings of anger, bitterness, and sadness? If so, you are not alone. Many individuals who have been wronged by their ex-spouse find it difficult to get beyond their painful experiences. One approach that can help you along the path toward emotional healing is forgiveness.

Forgiveness involves letting go of negative thoughts, feelings, or behaviors toward an offender (in this case, your ex-spouse) and taking a more positive approach. Forgiveness is NOT the same as forgetting what happened, condoning your ex-spouse's actions, giving up claims to a fair legal settlement, or reconciliation. While forgiveness may have benefits for others, it first and foremost can help you.

When deciding whether or not you wish to forgive, it is worth considering the growing body of scientific literature showing how hostility and forgiveness relate to your physical health, mental health, parenting style, and children's adjustment to divorce.

	Hostility	Forgiveness
Your Health	Hostility relates to chronic health problems such as coronary heart disease and high blood pressure	Forgiveness is associated with decreased physiological distress.
Your Happiness	Hostility is related to increased depression.	Forgiveness is associated with decreased depression.
Your Adjustment to Divorce	Hostility has been linked to poor coping strategies.	Forgiveness of an ex-spouse relates to better post-divorce adjustment.
Parenting and Your Children's Adjustment	Hostility can result in high conflict coparenting. Children often feel like they are stuck in the middle when their parents argue. Moreover, they might mimic any observed expressions of hostility in their own relationships.	Forgiveness relates to improved coparenting and less parental conflict. Modeling forgiveness for your children may help them consider this as a strategy when they experience interpersonal conflict in the future.

Forgiveness is challenging

While there are important benefits associated with forgiveness, there are obstacles that can make it difficult to forgive. Having an awareness of these challenges can help you to overcome them when they arise. Forgiveness is especially difficult when:

- The transgression was severe
- The offender did not apologize
- You are involved in ongoing legal and/or financial disputes
- You are experiencing significant conflict related to parenting

Steps toward forgiveness

If you are willing to work through these obstacles and pursue forgiveness, you might want to consider the steps involved in the process. A psychologist by the name of Everett Worthington has proposed five steps toward forgiveness that can be summarized with the acronym REACH.

- **Recall the hurt.** It is important to fully experience the emotions related to wrongdoing before moving forward. It is also helpful to express these feelings to people you can trust.
- **Empathize with the offender.** Empathy makes it easier to forgive. Try to think of alternative explanations for your ex's behavior and the ways that s/he may be suffering. Although this may be difficult at first, it can help you move beyond your negative feelings.
- **Altruistic gift.** Some people find it helpful to think about forgiveness as a gift that will benefit others. For instance, think about the possible benefits that forgiveness might have for your children, family, or mutual friends. Some people even hope that forgiveness can benefit their ex-spouse. Although this step in the model focuses on the altruistic nature of your decision to forgive, we would like to add that forgiveness can also be viewed as a gift to yourself that enables you to release the chains that bind you to toxic feelings.
- **Commitment to forgive.** Forgiveness is a process that starts with a commitment. To signify this important step, you might develop a creative way to mark your decision. This could involve using your artistic abilities (e.g., expressing your decision through art, music, or creative writing), talking about your decision with others, or developing a ritual (e.g., letting go of helium balloons) to signify you are ready to let go of painful feelings.
- **Hold on to forgiveness.** Because forgiveness is a process, you can sometimes experience setbacks. This happens to most people, so try not to be so hard on yourself about it. Some of the tips below may help you to hold onto forgiveness.

Tips for holding on to forgiveness

- **Reframe your situation.** Recognize that you cannot control your ex-'s behavior but you can control how you think and respond! Try to reframe the wrongdoing and view these events as an opportunity for personal growth.
- **The unmailed letter.** For this exercise, write a letter to your ex- in which you express whatever you want to say without censoring yourself. The letter should NOT be sent because this could add "fuel to the fire" and make your situation worse. Instead, view this as an opportunity to reflect upon the hurtful feelings that resulted from your divorce.

- **Daily affirmations.** Some people find that daily affirmations can help with forgiveness. Consider looking for inspiring quotes about forgiveness or healing and reflecting upon them each day. Place them in a location where you are sure to see them (e.g., refrigerator, bathroom mirror) and repeat them to yourself during times of need.
- **Spiritual coping.** Prayer, meditation and other spiritual strategies may be helpful if you are a spiritual person. A spiritual framework can provide justifications for forgiveness, role models for forgiveness, and inspiring scripture passages that encourage you along the forgiveness path.
- **Improve communication with your ex.** Some people have to continue communicating with their ex- about parenting or other issues. If this is true for you, consider the following tips for improving communication:
    (1) Do not have any discussions while angry.
    (2) Do not verbally attack the other person.
    (3) Turn accusatory messages into "I messages" so that your ex- better understands your feelings and is less likely to become defensive. For instance, rather than saying "You never pick up the kids on time" consider saying "When you are late picking up the kids, I become frustrated because I have to rearrange my work schedule."
    (4) When speaking, reflect back the person's perspective, even if you disagree. Then calmly explain how you disagree.
    (5) Siphon out the nastiness in your communications, even if your ex- will not do the same.

Self-forgiveness

During the complicated and emotionally challenging process of getting divorced, people sometimes act in ways they later regret. In fact, the intense guilt, regret, and shame about one's own actions can be incredibly painful and distressing. If you can relate to these feelings, you might consider working on self-forgiveness.

- Self-forgiveness is the process of letting go of your shame and regret and replacing these feelings with compassion, generosity, and love for yourself.xiv

- Self-forgiveness does NOT involve excusing your behavior or ignoring your mistakes. You have to first accept responsibility for your own hurtful actions before you begin to forgive yourself.xv
- You do not need to wait to be forgiven for your own hurtful actions in order to start forgiving yourself.

Information and guidance provided by Mark S. Rye, Ph.D. and the Skidmore College Positive Psychology Research team. You may contact Dr. Rye by email at mrye@skidmore.edu.

Dr. Mark S. Rye is a clinical psychologist and Associate Professor of Psychology at Skidmore College. He has been researching and writing about forgiveness since 1996. Members of his research team are undergraduate students at Skidmore College.

Additional Resources

Additional resources and references for this Smart Guide may be found on pages 97-100.

Legal Separation – The Power of Setting Proper Expectations

The problems that caused the separation don't go away after separation. Communication problems with your co-parent are enhanced, not decreased, after separation.

Some people have unrealistic expectations about divorcing. While they have a feeling that the legal separation process may not be easy, they believe that the legal system will fix their problems and finally make their spouse behave properly. They often think that getting rid of that spouse will set the stage for happiness and a great relationship with someone else.

No matter how much you think that your separation will fix your problems, the things that made you want to run away from your spouse will still be there after separation. These things even frequently become a bigger problem after separation because the little goodwill that may have existed because you lived together is no longer present.

People also have the notion that their lawyers will be the guardians of their well being and will encourage them to take the appropriate actions along the way.

What they forget is that lawyers are supposed to take instructions from their clients, not the other way around. If clients instruct their lawyers from a place of anger, fear, insecurities and revenge chances are the recovery from the separation will take even longer.

Separating from a place of anger, resentment, hurt and revenge will fail everyone in the family and will keep people in the past. However actually addressing these feelings has the potential to enable the spouses to actually create their family of the future that is empowered, successful and in which each member of the family thrives.

This Smart Guide will expose some common false expectations that often lead to more hurt and disappointment, and will provide strategies for addressing these expectations.

Who People are When They Separate

There are three periods to consider when discussing separations: the pre-separation stage, the legal separation period, and the post-separation future. I invite you to reflect on what you can do to get through this as powerfully as possible. It is true that you will not have control over many things, but you will always have control over who you are and how you behave.

People in the pre-separation stage are generally unhappy, lonely and frustrated. They have a sense of failure towards themselves, their parents, social networks, and towards their partner and children. People who decide to separate have usually spent years trying to find solutions to the growing sense of loneliness and misalignment with their spouse. They have experienced being nervous about the future, being insecure about how they will make it financially, and they are frequently emotionally depleted from years of unhappiness.

Spouses who are willing to look at their part in the breakdown usually are more serene and realistic about what it will take to create their life after separation. They may not have all of the answers but they know that there is work to do. They may even feel euphoric at the prospect of being able to start again in the future. Spouses who are hurt, fragile, insecure and disempowered, and who feel that the separation is being imposed on them unfairly, will need extra help and time to grasp what is happening and to be able to be full participants in the creation of the separation and the post-separation period.

During the legal separation period, who people are is usually a function of how they were during the pre-separation stage. The more accepting people are of the separation, the better the chances of being aware and conscious of the choices that they will have to make during the legal separation period.

The risk is that if people enter the legal separation period from a place of fear, regret, anger and resentments, they risk creating a negative atmosphere and even make agreements and decisions that do not reflect who they really are and what they really want for their ex partner and their children. They may look back afterwards and not feel good about their legal separation results. Bitter divorces are also more expensive because it takes much longer to get through the process than if there is cooperation. Usually, people who are not doing well during the legal separation period will need much longer to adapt to their new circumstances and the healing process will take longer.

Who people are in the post-separation future depends on who they have been during the first two periods. People who expected the separation to fix things for them will be left feeling incomplete, resentful and insecure. They will experience life in the same way as during their dissatisfying marriage because the players are the same and their interactions and ways of communicating with each other will be the same. People who have taken the time to set themselves up powerfully with proper expectations, preparation and an open mind, will be set up to embrace the future and access more quickly the healing that is available during that period.

People who are not coping well are invited to find the resources that will enable them to face what lies ahead with as much grace and maturity as is possible. This is imperative for the sake of their children, their family and themselves.

Going through the legal separation process is harder than people imagine. People will be asked to provide instructions to their lawyer and to strategize about the outcomes that they want to achieve. If they instruct their lawyers from a place of anger, hurt and insecurity, they risk making mistakes and creating situations that they will regret.

The stronger people are during the first two periods, the better they will be able to set up themselves for the post-separation future, in a way that will reflect who they really are.

Creating Proper Expectations

Areas that were difficult or unmanageable during the marriage will continue to exist and probably even expand during the legal separation process.

I will now describe a series of situations that are likely to surprise you. These are situations that my clients misunderstood and which caught them off guard until it was too late in the process. When people are not prepared for situations and are caught off guard, they may experience a loss of power, frustration, anger and resentment. These feelings may cause people to react impulsively or negatively and may cause clients to provide instructions to their lawyer that will not be beneficial to themselves and their children on a long term basis. My goal is to expose difficult situations and allow you to get prepared to deal with them powerfully.

You may not get justification during your legal separation

People who separate are often preoccupied with their partner's faults and what their partners have done to them. They hope that the "legal system" will make them right and their ex wrong. This rarely happens. The legal system is preoccupied with creating finality rather than ascribing fault. The legal system is ill equipped to deal with the complexities of managing separated families.

Sometimes clients feel as if they have been wronged by their partner's conduct and because of how the law applies to them. There is not much the legal system or your lawyer can do about this.

Clients also often have unrealistic expectations about how their ex will behave during the legal separation process. They sometimes are shocked that their spouse is not accepting what they are proposing, or that their reasonable proposals are met with anger and stonewalling. But you need to realize that separations do not change your spouse's personality.

Areas that were difficult or unmanageable during the marriage will continue to exist and probably even expand during the legal separation process. Communication problems will persist during your legal separation process. This is why separation methods such as Collaborative Law and Mediation, which encourage the creation of a lasting working relationship post-separation, are valuable. Clients feel more comfortable with the shortcomings of the law and the legal process when they feel that their lawyer has represented them with humanity, respect and professionalism.

No one wins in Court

Court is a lose/lose proposition. Clients are often told by their lawyers that they have a good case based on the legal principles disclosed by the clients at the outset. What is missing from clients' understanding is the reality of several financial and non-financial costs associated with litigation.

What is not possible to assess at the outset of a case includes[1]:

- how long it will take to resolve the file because the court system is extremely slow
- how much opposition will be received from the other party and the other party's lawyer
- how the dynamic between the two lawyers involved will impact the case (positively or negatively)
- how much participants and children suffer emotionally as a result of the prolonged conflict
- how much productivity is affected by the prolonged conflict, such as time off work for document preparation, court attendances and the potential health effects associated with the stress of going through this adversarial process

At the end of the litigation process, it is highly likely that your relationship with your former partner will be permanently damaged, beyond your imagination.

You may not like how the law applies to you

The law is not very adaptable. It's fairly set and rigid. Some of you will experience great resistance at the state of the law. Frequent examples are that support payers resent having to pay

> It is rare that the two spouses will be at the same stage of acceptance of the separation at the same time.

support or disagree with the amount they have to pay. Stay at home parents resent needing to re-think their occupation to increase their income and/or being financially dependent on the other spouse.

Lawyers do not have the mandate to be preoccupied with their clients' well being

Lawyers have historically adopted adversarial attitudes because the system promoted "winners" and "losers". Our family law legal system is based on the notion that each party has separate and opposed rights which should be protected by their lawyers. Lawyers have a professional obligation to take in consideration and to "fight for" their clients' rights.

The lawyers' Code of Professional conduct does not enjoin lawyers to also be preoccupied with the well being of their clients. If that were the case, several lawyers would be disbarred. People's emotions and well being are not in the domain of divorce law.

Your shared parenting plan may be harder to implement than you think

No matter how well intentioned the spouses are, they will frequently experience differences in their parenting styles when they have established two residences. Children will quickly get the differences and may use them to their advantage!

Parenting post-separation requires more work than during the marriage. You are advised to consult professional help to get tips on how to make your co-parenting plan work well post separation.

Your legal separation may take a long time to complete / may come too fast

If you are the person who wanted the separation, chances are you are ready to go. You want the legal separation to be concluded as soon as possible, because you want to move on.

If you are the person upon whom a separation is imposed, you will need more time to adapt to the idea. The system will push you to embark on the legal separation. You will potentially find that things move too fast.

It is rare that the two spouses will be at the same stage of acceptance of the separation at the same time. Usually the person who wanted the separation will be further ahead in the stages of detachment than the person who was just told about the separation. The stage partners are at during the legal separation process will impact the pace of the process.

For example, it may be very difficult for a person who is in denial about the separation to participate actively in a negotiation session in which the topic of selling the matrimonial home will be discussed. A spouse who experiences some deep sadness or depression may not be capable of generating creative solutions to the issue of post-separation parenting.

A legal separation may go as fast as the slower of the two partners.

This does not mean that one has to wait forever for the other person to be ready to take on the next step in the legal separation. It does however mean that you and your lawyer must be mindful of the emotions of the two spouses and that your strategies and expectations are set accordingly. If you are in Court you will not have much control over the speed of the process; it has the potential to move extremely slowly. If you are in negotiation[2] you will have more control over the speed of the process. The timing and duration of meetings can accommodate the parties and what they need at every step.

Mature lawyers may guide you through the psychological aspects of your separation and help you manage the speed respectfully and appropriately.

You may receive conflicting advice

Undoubtedly your friends will want to help you and give you "advice" regarding your separation. It's similar to when you have children and everyone tells you how to be a parent. While your friends will mean well, some of this advice will be useful but some will definitively not be. Your friends only have a partial understanding of your life and unless they practice family

> People have the notion that once they get rid of their spouse, things will be ok. But who they have to co-parent with is the same person.

law, they DO NOT know the legal implications of your circumstances. The fact that friends also have kids does not mean that you will develop the same parenting schedule. The fact that their spouse may be a stay-at-home parent and that they make a similar salary to you will not necessarily mean that your spousal support arrangement will look similar.

You will need to use your own judgment to craft your own vision of what you want for your future.

You may not have the funds to pay for your lawyer

Many people can't fund the cost of the legal process out of their incomes, as they are barely keeping afloat. While you will need to plan to pay for your separation, you will be faced with the challenge that it is impossible to estimate how much it will cost. The cost will depend on several factors including:

- complexity of the issues
- conflict management
- personalities of the parties involved (spouses and their lawyers)
- influence of external forces (Who is really driving the file: a parent, a new partner, a cheerleading group of friends, and a support group?)

Before embarking on your legal separation process, you may benefit from seeking financial advice from trusted sources (such as financial planners, knowledgeable parents) to help you plan the funding of your separation. This will diminish the stress you would otherwise encounter every time you get a bill from your lawyer or other experts involved in your file!

Once you separate, you will be rid of all of your problems

People have the notion that once they get rid of their spouse, things will be ok. But who they have to co-parent with is the same person. Who they have to discuss their children's education is the same person. Who they have to discuss summer camps and extracurricular programs with is the same person. Who they have to discuss funding their kids' programs with is the same person. A separation will not make our ex into a better person. We suggest you develop strategies with your lawyer that will incorporate your former partner's personalities.

Our legal system is not designed to take into account the complex emotional and practical needs of families and children. You need to be the guardian of your own welfare because chances are no one else will do that for you.

Setting proper expectations and addressing the feelings of resentment and hurt that are often present at the time of separation, is the basis for the creation of a powerful post-separation family. You owe it to yourself, your ex partner and your children to empower yourself for success during this challenging experience.

[1] Inspired by *The New Lawyer: How Settlement is Transforming the Practice of Law* by Julie MacFarlane, UBC

[2] *Negotiation can be:* One On One Negotiation, Mediation, Collaborative Law, or Unregulated Lawyer Negotiation

Information and guidance provided by Nathalie Boutet
You may contact Ms. Boutet by e-mail at -
nboutet@boutetfamilylaw.com

Nathalie Boutet is a leading Canadian family law lawyer. She is also a Deputy Judge in the Ontario Small Claims Court, a local and international teacher and she is a sought after Mediator and Collaborative Law lawyer. She regularly provides opinions to the Media on current legal matters.

Understanding Your Divorce Options

When you and your partner separate, you will need to deal with different legal matters. You will need to have a separation agreement that sets out the terms for spousal support, child care, and division of family property and assets, among other matters. There are two ways to formalize your legal separation:

1. If you can stay out of court, you will likely sign a separation agreement
2. If you are unable to arrive at an agreement on your own, and the matter goes to court, then you will obtain a divorce decree (the Court's formal order for granting the termination of a marriage.)

Many family issues over financial support, the care of your children, parenting plan, and the division of assets can be resolved without going to court. Taking matters to court can be expensive, time-consuming and stressful, and may take away any control or certainty over the outcome that you had hoped for.

Your first step is to familiarize yourself with all of the divorce options available to you. It is important to know something about the dispute resolutions before you meeting with a lawyer because some lawyers will not tell you bout options that they do not practice. What ever divorce process you choose to pursue, it is essential for you to consult with your lawyer before you commit to any process or sign a separation agreement, and to clearly understand:

- The divorce/separation process, your legal rights and obligations.
- What personality or emotional issues might surface, and what process is best suited to deal with these issues.
- Who will have control over making decisions — for example, a judge, a neutral third party, or you and your spouse
- The costs associated with the process.

A smart divorce involves taking the time to explore your options and to clearly outline your family situation so that you and your family law lawyer can evaluate which divorce process is most appropriate for protecting the best interests of your children and yourself in the context of your goals for separation while maintaining your sanity and dignity.

Here, then, are the divorce processes, what they are, how they work, and what to consider.

Alternative Dispute Resolution

Alternative Dispute Resolution (ADR) involves resolving issues or disputes in ways other than going to court. Talk to your lawyer, before you agree to any type of ADR process to make sure that you do not give up rights that you may be unaware that you have. There are four types of ADR that can be used for family law disputes: negotiation, mediation, arbitration and collaborative family law.

Negotiation

In a negotiation process, each party with the help of their lawyer, prepares a proposal that he or she believes is fair and shares it with the other party. The proposal would include such matters as spousal and child support, parenting responsibilities, visitation rights and division of family assets and liabilities. These proposals are considered the starting point. The parties would go back and forth, on their own, through lawyer's letters or round table meetings, negotiating respective positions and proposals, and adjusting until an acceptable middle ground is reached.

The negotiation process is used in mediation, Collaborative

Family Law, and in most cases within the litigation process, in order to help prevent the need for an actual trial.

Mediation

In mediation, you and your spouse work together to talk about and resolve the problems arising from your separation with the help of a neutral third-party, a mediator. Usually the mediator is a lawyer, mental health or other trained professional.

A mediator cannot give you legal advice but may give you general information about family law. Before you hire a mediator, you and your spouse should get independent legal advice from your own lawyers to ensure that you fully understand your rights and obligations, what is fair and acceptable to negotiate, whether your mediation should be closed or confidential mediation, or open or recommending mediation, and the considerations around this. Closed or confidential mediation is mediation where no input is given to the system by the mediator if the divorcing couple does not come to an agreement. Open or recommending mediation is a form of mediation where the mediator may issue a report and in fact recommendations if the divorcing couple cannot come to agreements. Your lawyer can also help you to prepare for the mediation and assist you in gathering the documents you will need.

> The mediator will not make decisions for you, but will help the two of you to make your own decisions.

The mediator will ask the couple to sign an agreement to mediate. Your lawyer can also help you to prepare for the mediation and assist you in gathering the documents you will need.

The mediator listens to what's important to both of you, asks for your opinions and views on the issues, and helps the two of you come to your own solutions about the future. The mediator will not make decisions for you, but will help the two of you to make your own decisions. In true mediation, what is called closed or confidential mediation you own the outcome. The mediator is a catalyst and agent of your creative agreement-making.

It is always a good idea to do your research in advance of

mediation to find the right mediator for your needs. For example, if you were developing a parenting plan, or had many child related issues you likely want your mediator to be a mental health professional – who is a parenting expert such as a psychologist or social worker. If on the other hand you had many financial issues, most lawyers would recommend you use a mediator who is a family law lawyer with a financial background. If necessary, you may need more than one mediator to deal with the different issues. Your lawyer or local bar association should be able to help refer you to mediators to interview so that you can find a good fit for you.

A mediator can suggest ways to solve the conflict, but you do not have to take their advice. If you are not happy with the mediation, you can leave and it will be over. If you cannot reach an agreement, the mediation will end. At that point, you could try a different kind of ADR, or go to court. If you come to an agreement at mediation, many lawyers suggest that you do not sign the separation agreement until you get the input of your advising lawyer.

Collaborative Family Law

Collaborative Family Law is a process of legal separation or divorce in which both parties and their collaborative family law lawyers pledge in writing to resolve all issues by agreement without the involvement of the Court.

Instead of engaging in an adversarial process, the focus is to maintain cooperation and open communication so that a settlement can be reached that meets the needs of all family members. Further, a goal for collaborative divorce is to directly assist the parties in their emotional healing, allowing them to more readily move forward into their new lives.

Collaborative divorce proceeds by assembling multidisciplinary teams that usually include collaboratively trained lawyers, a neutral financial professional and collaboratively trained mental health professionals. When divorcing parties meet, their teams are by their sides to help them conduct negotiations based on what they need, not necessarily just on rights and entitlement, and to work towards a parenting and financial plan that is acceptable to both clients. If either client wishes to end the collaborative process and go to court, all team members must remove themselves from the case and the parties must retain new divorce professionals.

When you participate in this process, both you and your spouse retain collaborative family law lawyers. Collaborative family lawyers have special training in collaborative practice. In addition to consulting privately with your collaborative family law lawyer, in some cases mental health coaches will participate individually with you and your spouse, and his or her collaborative family law lawyer and other members of your collaborative team. Your lawyer is directly involved in discussions with your spouse and his or her counsel. This offers your lawyer a unique opportunity, unavailable in any other resolution process, to develop an understanding of both parties' positions, which opens up further opportunities for discussion and settlement.

The goal is to allocate the financial resources of the family and to restructure the parenting obligations and responsibilities of both spouses in a non-confrontational and balanced manner that has a positive outcome for the family. Other professionals such as financial planners, accountants, parenting specialists, family counsellors, and divorce coaches, can be brought in to assist in the resolution process as required.

Sometimes, couples cannot reach a mutually agreeable separation agreement during the process. If either spouse wants to end the collaborative process and go to Court, you must each hire a new lawyer to represent you in Court.

While there are many benefits to collaborative law, it is something that not all lawyers are supportive of; nor is it practiced in all states or provinces. If you decide to pursue this route, make sure the lawyers you consult with are collaborative trained lawyers.

Arbitration

Arbitration is a process in which both spouses and your lawyers hire an arbitrator to decide the issues in question. The arbitrator is usually a retired judge or senior lawyer with a family law background. Arbitrators can only decide on the family law matters that you ask them to resolve.

It is essential that you talk to a lawyer to ensure that you are fully informed of your legal rights and obligations, and how the arbitration process works. Once arbitration begins, you cannot walk away. Once both sides of the case are presented to the arbitrator, it is his or her job to reach a decision on the issues presented. The arbitration will end with a judgement and you will receive an arbitration award. This is the document that sets out the arbitrator's decisions. Arbitration awards can sometimes be difficult to enforce, so it may be preferable to turn it into a court order.

Keep in mind: arbitration is not the same as mediation. In mediation, you have choices. You can choose to end the mediation, or decide not to accept what your spouse is offering or what the mediator suggests. In arbitration, the arbitrator has the control. The arbitrator's decision is usually binding and enforceable as long as it follows the law, and generally cannot be appealed. If you are considering arbitration, before you agree to the process, consult with your lawyer to ensure that you are fully informed of what you are getting into.

Despite these limitations, many lawyers prefer arbitration to the less desirable alternative of a costly, protracted, public court battle — with the arbitration process, you have some degree of control over the selection of the judge/decision-maker, and because there is no public record of the dispute, your family's privacy is protected.

You will need to consult with your lawyer to find out if the option of arbitration is available in your province or state of jurisdiction.

Do-It-Yourself Divorce

A "do-it-yourself" divorce in legal terms is called Divorce Pro Se or pro per or "self representation". The divorcing couple draws up their own separation agreement, without the help of a lawyer, and presents it to a judge to sign.

This option requires a high level of trust, communication, cooperation, and complete financial disclosure between both parties, if the outcome is to be successful.

Some people do an excellent job of drawing up their own agreement. However, other separating couples fail to represent

> If each side's tactic is to try to make the other look bad, the impact on the family can be disastrous and may destroy the possibility of any kind of amicable relationship later on.

themselves wisely. Consider that divorce is not about saving money, but rather it's about protecting your children's and your own best interests. This is why, many lawyers advise against this approach: even for those who research and become familiar with their rights and responsibilities. The legal, financial and emotional issues can easily get in the way. Attempting to navigate child-related issues, as well as pension, tax, and other financial matters without experienced professionals involved could put you and your children in a vulnerable — and possibly — regrettable situation.

If you do decide that this option is for you, know that some people before proceeding choose to seek independent legal advice (ILA) to understand their legal rights and obligations, and then check with their lawyer again before signing the separation agreement. It is essential that both you and your soon to be ex-spouse consult with your own respective lawyers to ensure that your best interests are being looked out for.

Litigation

Litigation is a process in which a controversy is presented to a Court and decisions are made by a judge, or in some states by a jury. Often referred to as the option of last resort, litigation is often referred to as an adversarial process.

In litigation, there is no separation agreement, or input by you and your spouse All decisions about your separation—including financial, child related or other matters are made by a judge. At the end of your trial, you will be given a divorce decree or divorce judgment by a Court of law.

Going to Court is an emotionally stressful and public process. You must be prepared for the exposure of the details of your life, and for the fact that there will be a record of the dispute. If each side's tactic is to try to make the other look bad, the impact on the family can be disastrous and may destroy the possibility of any kind of amicable relationship later on.

There are times, however, when going to Court may be unavoidable. This might be the case, for example, if one partner threatens to hide or destroy assets, take the children out of town, or refuses to pay child support. Other issues that can lead to litigation include disputes over child support, child custody, spousal support, alimony, and division of family property and assets.

In addition to being an emotionally charged and stressful experience, litigation is very expensive. Litigators charge by the hour in family law cases, and this does not include fees, deposition costs and other expenses related to bringing the case to Court, which are also charged to you. There are rules of procedure that govern how a case is processed through court. Many states have gone a step further and adopted rules of procedure specific to family law.

Of all the cases that end up in Court, approximately 3% of these go all the way to a full-blown trial. Some lawyers use the threat of trial to get people to bargain and settle. It is always a good idea to negotiate and to attempt to settle if possible.

Going to Court can seem like an eternity, as it takes time to get to trial. There is a set process that needs to be followed, and it can take months or even years to finally reach a resolution. Talk to your lawyer to get a sense of the emotional side of litigation. This is also a good time to turn to your therapist or a trusted confidant for emotional support.

Other Considerations

The information presented here provides a basic overview of the divorce settlement options and should be discussed with your lawyer. Be aware that whatever process you choose, your lawyer cannot control how your spouse will behave, who he or she will hire, or whether common sense will prevail. Ultimately, your goal should be to choose a divorce process to end the marriage as reasonably and amicably as possible while protecting the wellbeing of you and your children.

Finding A Good Divorce Lawyer

Choosing the right lawyer may be the most important decision in ending your marriage and successfully beginning the next phase of your life. Although it takes time and effort to find the right lawyer, you owe it to yourself to choose carefully and to find a divorce lawyer who will be your advocate and an asset throughout your divorce process, so that you and your family can come out of this with your sanity and dignity intact. You need to find an experienced and competent lawyer with whom you feel comfortable, and trust to protect your children's best interests, as well as your own, for the long haul. So where do you begin? Use the following smart divorce strategies to choose the right lawyer for you, to ask important questions, to manage the consult, and to have a clear understanding of how to work effectively together.

Conduct an informed search

First things first: you need to look for a lawyer whose expertise is in family law. There are many issues particular to family law. Experience and competency in this area matter. You need a divorce lawyer who appreciates the impact of divorce on the family, who understands the legal and emotional intricacies of a parenting plan, and who is well versed in the particulars of spousal support, extraordinary child expenses, and all aspects of financial disclosure.

Build a list of qualified candidates

You should not expect to find a good family law lawyer simply by looking in the phonebook or online. A much better approach is to build a list of qualified divorce lawyers. There are a number of ways to do this. Keep in mind that you should never make a decision to hire a lawyer simply on the basis of someone else's recommendation. It's important that you meet the lawyer, ask lots of questions and then carefully assess whether the lawyer is the right fit for you. But, be aware that not all lawyers practice in Alternative Dispute Resolution (ADR) such as Collaborative Family Law or mediation, so might not recommend these friendlier processes. Consider interviewing at least three lawyers before you make your decision about who to retain.

> Keep in mind that you should never make a decision to hire a lawyer simply on the basis of someone else's recommendation.

Personal referrals. Divorce is common. Ask friends and family who have gone through divorce if they know a good lawyer. Ask questions to learn what their experience was like and what were the strengths and weaknesses of their lawyer. You might also ask who the former spouse retained, who they felt was the better lawyer, and why.

Business and legal referrals. You may be working with an accountant, financial planner, investment manager, banker, or even a legal professional who has regular contact with family law lawyers.

Family and mental health practitioner referrals. Your family doctor or therapist may be able to suggest family lawyers who have helped clients with similar backgrounds and circumstances to your own.

Employer referrals. Your company may have an Employee Assistance Program (EAP) that can provide you with a confidential referral to a family law lawyer.

Bar Association referrals. Every province and state has a bar association for lawyers. Most will refer you to a lawyer near where you live who is licensed to practice in that province or state and who specializes in divorce law.

Online research. If you are unable to get a referral to a lawyer through someone you know, there are many legal web sites that provide lawyer referrals. You will need to carefully check out the reputation of each firm. If there is a legal firm that you are familiar with that has an excellent reputation, you can review the firm's website including checking the biographies of some of the younger lawyers in the firm whose hourly rates may be more affordable and who may be supervised by highly regarded senior lawyers within the firm.

Interview Potential Lawyers

Once you have the names of several good prospects, the next step is to set up an initial interview with at least three lawyers. An initial interview is called a consultation. Before you set this up, ask if there is a fee. Some lawyers are willing to meet with you, for a half hour or so, at no charge for the consult so that you can assess whether the potential lawyer is a good candidate for you. This is also an opportunity in advance of the consultation, to prepare a brief outline of your situation and your needs in advance. Try to keep this as a concise, objective, honest description of the situation with your spouse, whether there are children involved, what type of agreement you have discussed so far, and whether there are any potential parenting, child custody and support, or financial issues.

Ask questions

Don't be afraid to interview your potential lawyer and to ask lots of questions to help evaluate which lawyer might be the right fit for you. They are also doing the same with you. Not every lawyer takes on every prospect that comes into their office. Prepare your questions in advance of the meeting, using the list below as a guideline. The questions and answers will also help you to work more effectively with your lawyer.

1. What is your approach to settling a case?

2. Do you have a preferred approach to dispute resolution?

3. How often do you go to court, and how often does this end in a trial (a decision made by a judge)?

4. Are you a family law lawyer? Are you certified as a family law specialist?

5. Do you practice in all of the divorce options (mediation, Collaborative Family Law, arbitration, or litigation)? Do you have a specialty or preference for settlement?

6. How many years have you been practicing family law?

7. What are my rights and obligations?

8. Do you believe the allegations coming from each side? Will you investigate them?

9. What is your hourly rate? What other expenses and costs should I expect? How do your billings and retainers work?

10. How will we communicate? E-mail, teleconference, or personal meetings?

11. What is your response time for returning phone calls, emails, and addressing issues?

12. Will I approve letters before they go out, and will you copy me on all letters going in and out?

13. Do you have the time for my case?

14. How do you settle cases and what is the process?

15. Have you handled a case like mine before and had similar issues? How did you handle it? Do you handle complex issues and how do you deal with them?

16. What strategy do you recommend I follow for financial issues? For child-related issues? Do we deal with each separately or at the same time, and why?

17. What is your philosophy of bringing in non lawyers (i.e. family counselors) into the process and others who may have expertise relating to the issues of the particular case?

Finding a Good Divorce Lawyer

18. Do you delegate some of the work to other individuals or juniors or do you do everything yourself?

19. Can I meet other members of your team?

20. What other professionals do you typically deal with and who are they?

21. What experience do you have dealing with personality disorder issues, or mental or physical abuse? (Ask this only if it's relevant to your own divorce.)

22. Are you teaching in the profession? Have you published any articles related to family law, and if so, where did these appear?

23. Do you have a recommended reading list or handouts?

24. Have you even been disciplined or disbarred by a bar association?

25. Have you or your insurance company paid on any malpractice claims? Do you carry malpractice insurance?

Assess qualifications and fit

Don't make the commitment to hire a lawyer at the consultation. This is an overwhelming time. You really need to think about the questions and answers after your meeting – then ask yourself "is this the right lawyer for me?" Your lawyer should have experience successfully handling the divorces of people with similar circumstances as you. Fees, costs and expenses should be fully disclosed, and you should be confident with the lawyer and the firm's qualifications and reputation. Pay particular attention to the approach and philosophy of your lawyer. No matter how well-recommended and experienced the lawyer may be, if you feel uncomfortable during the first few meetings, you need to trust your instincts and find a lawyer who has both the experience and approachability that you need. Think carefully about the costs. You need to find a lawyer within your budget.

If you feel uncomfortable during the first few meetings, you need to trust your instincts and find a lawyer who has both the experience and approachability that you need.

Take the time to search for the lawyer that

is right for you. In family law it is not uncommon for people to switch lawyers. If you feel that you have made a bad choice or a wrong choice, get a second opinion – especially before you sign a document. A second opinion is a good way to address and overcome your concerns.

Some people are intimidated by their lawyer and feel like they shouldn't ask questions. If you can't converse with you lawyer and don't have the comfort level, you might not get the answers you are seeking.

Going through a divorce can be challenging. Having a good lawyer on your side can make all the difference. By using these smart strategies and resources, you should be able to locate a lawyer who can guide you through the process, and help you get the results that you are looking for.

Understanding How Assets Get Divided In Divorce

Dividing the family's property during divorce can be quite difficult, especially if there are significant assets such as houses, rental property, retirement and pension plans, stock options, restricted stock, deferred compensation, brokerage accounts, closely-held businesses, professional practices and licenses, etc. Deciding who should get what can be quite a challenge, even under the most amenable of situations. But, if your divorce is contentious, then this can be especially complicated.

Assets should not necessarily be divided simply based on their current dollar value. You need to understand which assets will be best for your short- and long-term financial security. This is not always easy to discern without a thorough understanding of the asset itself – its liquidity, cost basis and any tax implications associated with its sale.

However, before we go any

Warning: Separate property can lose its separate property status if you commingle it with marital property or vice versa. For example, if you re-title your separately owned condo by adding your spouse as a co-owner or if you deposit the inheritance from your parents into a joint bank account with your spouse, then that property will most likely now be considered marital property.

further, we need to discuss the differences between Separate and Marital Property and why that's critically important to you. States differ in some of the details, but generally speaking, Separate Property includes:

- Any property that was owned by either spouse prior to the marriage;
- An inheritance received by the husband or wife (either before or after the marriage); a gift received by the husband or wife from a third party (your mother gave you her diamond ring);
- Payment received for pain and suffering portion in a personal injury judgment

All other property that is acquired during the marriage is usually considered marital property regardless of which spouse owns the property or how the property is titled. Most people don't understand this. I've had many clients tell me that they were not entitled to a specific asset, because it was titled in their spouse's name – such as their 401K. This is not true! This is worth repeating because it is that important. All property that is acquired during the marriage is usually considered marital property regardless of which spouse owns the property or how that property is titled.

(State laws vary greatly, especially between Community Property & Equitable Distribution States, so please consult with your lawyer).

Marital property consists of all income and assets acquired by either spouse during the marriage including, but not limited to: Pension Plans; 401Ks, IRAs and other Retirement Plans; Deferred Compensation; Stock Options; Restricted Stocks and other equity; bonuses; commissions; Country Club memberships; annuities; life insurance (especially those with cash values); Brokerage Accounts - mutual funds, stocks, bonds, etc; Bank Accounts - checking, savings, Christmas club, CDs, etc; closely-held businesses; professional practices and licenses; real estate; limited partnerships; Cars, boats, etc; art, antiques; tax refunds.

In many states, if your separately owned property increases in value during the marriage, that increase is also considered marital property. However some states will differentiate between active and passive appreciation when deciding if an

Marital property can include:
- Pension Plans; 401Ks, IRAs and other Retirement Plans
- Deferred Compensation
- Stock Options
- Restricted Stocks and other equity
- Bonuses
- Commissions
- Country Club memberships
- Annuities
- Life Insurance (especially those with cash values)
- Brokerage Accounts - mutual funds, stocks, bonds, etc
- Bank Accounts - Checking, Savings, Christmas Club, CDs
- Closely-held businesses
- Professional Practices and licenses
- Real Estate
- Limited Partnerships
- Cars, boats, etc
- Art, antiques
- Tax refunds

increase in the value of separate property should be considered marital property.

So what's the difference?

Active appreciation is appreciation that is due, in part, to the direct or indirect contributions or efforts of the other spouse (e.g. your spouse helped you grow your business by giving you ideas and advice; he/she entertained clients with you; he/she helped raise the kids and did some household chores, which allowed you to work late, entertain clients, travel to conventions; etc.).

Passive appreciation is appreciation that is due to outside forces such as supply and demand and inflation. For example, a parcel of land increases in value even though you and your husband made no improvements to it. However, if you used marital income and/or assets to pay the mortgage and/or taxes on this parcel of land, you might have a very good argument that this property, or at least the increase in value during your marriage, should now be considered marital property. As you can see, this can get quite complicated and convoluted. Hiring a good divorce financial planner can help you sort this out.

It is also very important for you to know if you reside in a Community Property State or an Equitable Distribution State. There are nine Community Property States - Arizona, California, Idaho, Louisiana, Nevada, New Mexico, Texas, Washington and Wisconsin. Community Property states consider both spouses as equal owners of all marital property (a 50-50 split is the rule).

The remaining 41 states are Equitable Distribution states. Settlements in Equitable Distribution States do not need to be equal, but they should be fair and equitable. In Equitable Distribution, several factors are taken into account, including the financial situation of each spouse when dividing assets.

Some of the factors considered are:

- The length of the marriage
- The income or property brought into the marriage by each spouse
- The standard of living established during the marriage
- The age and physical/emotional health of each spouse
- The income and earning potential of each spouse
- The financial situation of each spouse when the divorce is finalized
- The contribution of a spouse to the education, training or earning power of the other

The needs of the custodial parent to maintain the lifestyle for the children

In addition to these, a court can consider any other factors that it feels might be relevant. This makes it very difficult, if not impossible, to predict the outcome. The bottom line here is that you want to stay out of court, if possible. There's a good reason why more than 95% of all divorces are ultimately settled out of court.

Also, please remember that debts usually get divided in divorce as well. However, Community Property states treat debt differently than Equitable Distribution states, so please make sure that you consult with an experienced divorce specialist.

This is a basic description of how assets get divided in divorce will help you as you are going through your divorce. But as you can see, this can be an extremely complicated process filled with unseen potholes. Having a competent divorce financial profes-

> The bottom line here is that you want to stay out of court, if possible. There's a good reason why more than 95% of all divorces are ultimately settled out of court.

sional on your team can help you get your fair share of the assets that you've worked so hard to accumulate. And, always check with your family law lawyer before you sign any documents.

Financial information and guidance provided by Jeffrey A. Landers.
You may contact Jeffrey by email at landers@bedrockdivorce.com

Jeffrey A. Landers, CDFA is a Divorce Financial Strategist™ and the founder of Bedrock Divorce Advisors, LLC (http://www.BedrockDivorce.com), a divorce financial strategy firm that exclusively works with women, who are going through, or might be going through, a financially complicated divorce. He also advises women business owners on what steps they can take now to "divorce-proof" their business in the event of a future divorce.

Getting Your Finances and Record Keeping Organized for Divorce

The uncoupling of a husband and wife can have significant financial impact. What was once an income shared by two is now divided to support two households. Figuring out how to divide your assets and to establish child support and/or spousal support, if applicable, should head up your list of what you need to focus on. Your ultimate goal is to achieve a fair division of assets, to obtain child support that is in the best interests of your children, and to achieve good results in an amicable manner. Separating financially after marriage is not easy, however it is easy to feel overwhelmed. With a smart divorce, the way to overcome this is to get involved and to get organized to help your lawyer do the best job possible for you and without incurring additional unnecessary billable hours.

Become financially aware during the divorce process

All lawyers agree on how important it is for their clients to be as financially aware as possible. Achieving financial clarity is the best way to learn your rights and obligations and to set out realistic expectations early in the divorce process. Once you have a handle on your financial situation, your lawyer can give you informed opinions based on fact, not on speculation. The more you can manage and organize your information for your lawyer and establish realistic financial goals, the more you can help reduce your lawyer's billable hours.

These are some of the issues you might cover during the process with your financial adviser:

- Get more involved in your finances. Know the basics—how to pay the bills and file the statements. Learn how your daily and monthly expenses are managed.
- Determine where the money is coming from and how it is applied toward your budget.
- Understand what assets you have in total and where they are.
- Identify all sources of income, as well as any debts or liabilities you and your spouse have, either jointly or separately.
- Determine what credit cards and lines of credit you may have, either jointly or separately.
- Identify health and insurance policies and coverage, and important legal documents such as Wills and Power of Attorney.
- Take part in setting up investments and registered savings such as retirement funds and children's educational plans. Identify who the beneficiaries are.

Consult with a financial expert

During the divorce process, you need to be careful and to protect yourself. The financial issues associated with divorce can be complex. Without proper guidance, you could find yourself in an adverse situation later on, when it is too late to do something about it. Your lawyer may recommend that you work with additional legal and financial experts either associated with their firm or from your own personal team of resources. These professional advisors may include a lawyer, financial planner, financial advisor, broker, Chartered Financial Analyst, forensic accountant or other expert.

Establish your own financial identity

If you do not have a credit rating, now is the time to start building one. (Note that credit cards only affect the credit rating of each card's principal holder; you may find yourself with no credit rating even if you and your spouse had joint credit card accounts.) Here are some considerations to start building your financial identity:

- If you are in the matrimonial home and your spouse has left, you might want to consider putting the household bills in your name. Make sure you pay these off on time and in full.
- Apply for your own credit card. If you are a first-time card holder, you can always start out with a small credit limit and gradually increase it as you regularly pay your bill on time and prove to be a good credit risk.
- Set up your own bank account and try not to go into overdraft; if you do, ensure that you pay this off on time.
- Establish a realistic budget
- Speak to your lawyer about closing joint bank accounts and joint credit cards

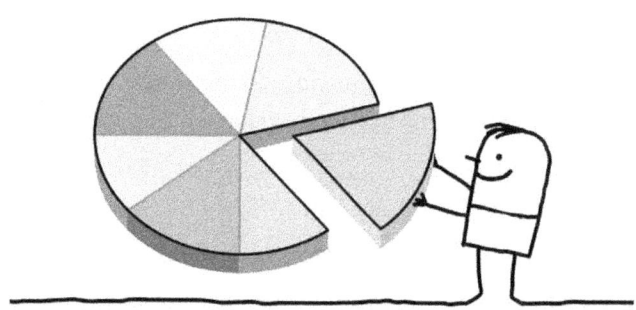

Get your financial documents in order

Make your legal consultation work for you, and start evaluating what is a reasonable outcome financially by bringing in as much financial information as possible. If you don't have this information for your consultation, make a significant effort to get it at the beginning of the divorce process when you have retained a lawyer. Once the divorce process is under way, your lawyer will need ready access to all relevant financial documents. Take control by getting your finances in order. Don't worry, your lawyer will help you strategize if you don't have access to the information. Start by locating and gathering the following records for you and your spouse:

- Social security numbers
- Income tax returns for the past three years
- Retirement savings plans statements for the past three years
- Bank account statements
- Insurance policies (life; automobile; house; other)
- Stock certificates
- Credit card bills
- Employment payment stubs
- Brokerage statements
- Pension statements
- Health insurance and work-related benefits
- Real estate records
- Receipts and monthly statements documenting household expenses and everyday expenses (groceries, gas, heat, water, personal grooming, transportation, gifts, clothing, laundry and cleaning supplies, entertainment, miscellaneous expenses, and so forth)
- List of all assets and liabilities
- Date of separation (the date of separation, or "valuation date," is the date that is used to determine the value of particular assets—the matrimonial home, bank statements, investments, and so forth)

> Photocopy everything, and store your set in a separate folder from the original records. Don't just keep the originals for your own personal use; the other side is entitled to these documents too.

Photocopy everything, and store your set in a separate folder from the original records. Don't just keep the originals for your own personal use; the other side is entitled to these documents too. If you do withhold these records, sooner or later you will be asked to provide them, which will cost you even more in legal fees.

Once the divorce process is underway, your lawyer will request your relevant financial documents. You will probably have to fill out a Financial Statement. The Financial Statement will be used to help establish your assets and liabilities for specific purposes – to determine marital property and support (child and spousal) claims. The Financial Statement sets out your income, expenses, assets and debts.

> Treat your divorce like a job: be organized.

Filling out your Financial Statement honestly and accurately is very important. The first page is a summary of your income, expenses, property and debts.

Photocopy all of the information and keep it in a safe place, perhaps a new safety deposit box or a trusted friend's house.

There are times when the information is impossible to find or you may be having a difficult time getting it from the other side. Before you spend money with your lawyer retrieving it, do your own fact finding – go to your banker, your broker, call the telephone company, and so forth to get the information you need to validate your assets, liabilities and expenses. The more financial information you can pass along to your lawyer, the better. You may also consult with your lawyer to help you strategize ways to obtain the information.

> In a high conflict situation, consider keeping a journal of events for your lawyer; and stay organized by keeping notes.

More ideas for organizing and record keeping

Treat your divorce like a job: be organized, set realistic expectations, do whatever work you can yourself in a timely way, take responsibility, and access as much information as possible.

If you're in the midst of a divorce, contemplating one or in a high conflict situation, consider keeping a journal of events for your lawyer; and stay organized by keeping notes. I am not suggesting that you should be starting off in an aggressive way, but for some people this information has been helpful. And, some people don't need this because there is a certain level of trust.

Divorce Journal. Note all events that involve you and your children that you feel are relevant to your divorce and that may affect the outcome. You and your lawyer may want to refer to this journal to help you confirm relevant dates and information. You might want to include affidavits, letters, and other written documents. This will help to show the accuracy of information and to validate dates, times, and other facts.

Meetings Notebook. Establish a notebook just for divorce. This will help keep you organized, and in control. Ensure that you follow up on your meeting notes and tasks assigned. To keep you organized; make certain that you date your notes. Divide your notebook into four sections:

- Meeting agendas and questions
- Notes from the meetings
- Next steps, or "to do" lists, with deadline dates, completion dates, and the date that each completed task or document was communicated or sent to my legal counsel
- Contacts, phone numbers, miscellaneous information

Divorce Filing System

Keep important documents accessible, organized, and together in one place. Your filing system does not have to be complicated or expensive. Consider using an expandable 31 day folder and file folders. Your filing system should include:

- All correspondence between you and your lawyer – make sure it is dated
- All invoices and statements –costs related to your divorce
- Any court orders or agreements which you are working through, or have agreed to and signed
- A folder for each member of your divorce team such as the financial expert, parenting expert, or others

The more you can manage and organize your information for your lawyer and establish realistic financial goals, the more you can help reduce your lawyer's billable hours.

- Your Financial Statement that your lawyer asks you to fill out
- Your parenting plan, if you have children
- If you are in the litigation process, all of the paperwork that you have collected

The more you can manage and organize your information for your lawyer and establish realistic financial goals, the more you can help reduce your lawyer's billable hours. Being organized will help reduce your stress and give you a sense of control.

Financial Information Checklist

Divorce requires you to be in charge of your money. This may, or may not, have been an area in your marriage where you either managed the money, or shared in the responsibility and decisions around your family finances. With your divorce, you are now taking back that power. If this is new territory for you, you might feel a little overwhelmed. To get past that fear and to take control, you need to both educate and prepare yourself for your financial independence.

Financial control helps to reduce your stress level and legal bills. One of the first steps to creating a financial snapshot of your situation is to fill out a financial statement. It's easy to find a template online. You can begin an online search by using the words "financial statement" and you should be able to find helpful guides. You are probably going to have to fill out a financial statement for your lawyer, so you might as well start working on your financial picture now. This will help you determine what your monthly budget is, and give your lawyer a more accurate picture of what your financial obligations and needs are, and the potential financial settlement.

To help fill out your financial statement, and gain an understanding of your finances, you may begin by collecting important financial documents.

Checklist of Important Financial Documents

☐ **1. Income Tax Returns.** Completed personal, corporate, partnership, joint venture, or other income tax returns (federal, state and local), including W-2, 1099, and K-1 forms, in your possession or control for the last 5 years, including all amended tax returns. Do you expect any tax refunds?

☐ **1A. Business Financial Statements.**

Net worth statement – balance sheet or list of assets and liabilities

Income statement – cash flow or income and expense statement

☐ **2. Income Information.** Current income information, including payroll stubs and all other evidence of income (investment property, rental/lease agreements, dividends, interest, royalties, lottery winnings, etc.) since the filing of your last tax return.

☐ **3. Personal Property Tax Returns** filed in this state or anywhere else from the start of the marriage.

☐ **4. Banking Information.** All monthly bank statements, passbooks, check registers, deposit slips, canceled checks, and bank charge notices on personal and business accounts, certificates of deposit, and money market and retirement accounts from banks, savings and loan institutions, credit unions, or other institutions in which you or your spouse has an interest.

☐ **5. Financial Statements.** All statement submitted to banks, lending institutions, or any other persons or entities, which were prepared by you or your spouse at any time during the last five (5) years.

☐ **6. Loan Applications.** Any loan applications made within the last five (5) years

☐ **7. Brokerage Statements.** Statements from all accounts of securities and/or commodities dealers or mutual funds maintained by you or your spouse during the marriage, and held individually, jointly, or as a trustee or guardian.

☐ **8. Stocks, Bonds and Mutual Funds.** Certificates, if available, of accounts owned by either spouse during the marriage or pre-owned by you.

☐ **9. Stock Options.** All records pertaining to stock options held in any corporation or other entity, exercised or not exercised (include any restricted stock).

☐ **10. Monetary Plans.** Pension, Money Purchase Plans, Profit Sharing, Employee Stock Option Plans, Deferred Compensation Agreement, and Retirement Plans (401 K, 403B, 412(e)(3), 457, military, IRA, Roth IRA, SEP-IRA, Keogh) or any other kind of plan owned by you or by any corporation in which you and/or your spouse have been a participant during the marriage, including annual statements.

☐ **11. Wills and Trust Agreements** (include any Powers of Attorney, etc.) executed by you or in which you have a present or contingent interest or in which you are a beneficiary, trustee, executor, or guardian and from which benefits have been received, are being received, or will be received and which are or were in existence during the past five (5) years, including inter vivos trusts. All records of declaration of trust and minute books for all trusts to which you are a party, including the certificates, if any, showing such interest and copies of all statements, receipts, disbursements, investments, and other transactions.

☐ **12. Insurance Policies.** Life Insurance or certificate of life insurance policies now in existence, insuring your life or the life of your spouse, and statements of the cash value, if available.

☐ **13. General Insurance.** Copies of insurance policies, including, but not limited to, annuities, health, accident, disability, casualty, motor vehicles of any kind, property liability, including contents, and insurance owned by the parties during the past five (5) years of the marriage.

☐ **14. Outstanding Debts.** Documents reflecting all debts owed to you or by you (including those cosigned by you), secured or unsecured, including mortgages, personal loans, credit card statements, promissory notes and lawsuits pending or previously filed in any court.

☐ **15. Business Records** or ledgers in your possession and control that are either personal or business-related, together with all accounts and journals.

☐ **16. Real Property.** Any deeds of property in which you and/or your spouse have an interest, together with evidence of all contributions, in cash or otherwise, made by you or on your behalf, toward the acquisition of such real estate during the marriage. Include all purchase agreements, mortgages, notes, property tax statements, rental/lease agreements, appraisals and all expenses associated with each property.

☐ **16A. Other real property.** List of real property owned prior to your marriage as well as real property acquired during the marriage by gift and/or inheritance.

☐ **17. Sale and Option Agreements** on any real estate owned by you either individually, through another person or entity, jointly, or as trustee or guardian.

☐ **18. Personal Property.** Documents, invoices, contracts, insurance policies, and appraisals on all personal property, including furniture, fixtures, jewelry, artwork, furnishings, furs, equipment, antiques, and any type of collections (coin, stamps, gold, etc.), owned by you individually, jointly, as trustee or guardian, or through any other person or entity during the term of themarriage.

☐ **18A. List of personal property owned prior to your marriage** as well as personal property acquired during the marriage by gift and/or inheritance.

☐ **19. Motor Vehicles.** All financing agreements and titles to all motor vehicles owned by you, individually or jointly, at any time during the last five (5) years, including airplanes, boats, automobiles, or any other types of motor vehicles.

☐ **20. Corporate Interests.** All records showing any kind of personal interest in any corporation (foreign or domestic) or any other entities not evidenced by certificate or other instrument.

☐ **21. Partnership and Joint Venture Agreements** to which you have been a party during the marriage.

☐ **22. Employment Records** during the term of the marriage, showing evidence of wages, salaries, bonuses, commissions, raises, promotions, expense accounts, and other benefits or deductions of any kind whether in cash, stock and/or other property. All records showing any fringe benefits available to you or your spouse from any business entity including, without limitation, auto, travel, private aircraft, boat, apartment/home, entertainment, country club, health club/spa, educational, vacation pay, severance pay, personal living expenses, etc.

☐ **23. Employment contracts** under which you or your spouse have performed services during the past five (5) years, including a list of description of any oral contracts.

☐ **24. Charge Account statements** for the past five (5) years.

☐ **25. Membership cards** or documents identifying participation rights in any country clubs, health clubs/spas, key clubs, private clubs, associations, or fraternal group organizations during the past five (5) years of the marriage, together with all monthly statements.

☐ **26. Judgments** and pleadings in which you have been a party to, either as Plaintiff or Defendant, during the marriage, including any Personal Injury Awards.

☐ **27. Asset appraisals.** Appraisals of any asset owned by you for the past five (5) years.

☐ **28. Safe Deposit Boxes.** Include a list of its contents.

☐ **29. Other.** Anything else that you think may be an asset.

Financial information and guidance provided by Jeffrey A. Landers.
You may contact Jeffrey by email at landers@bedrockdivorce.com

Jeffrey A. Landers, CDFA is a Divorce Financial Strategist™ and the founder of Bedrock Divorce Advisors, LLC (http://www.BedrockDivorce.com), a divorce financial strategy firm that exclusively works with women, who are going through, or might be going through, a financially complicated divorce. He also advises women business owners on what steps they can take now to "divorce-proof" their business in the event of a future divorce.

The Important Financial Steps Required to Prepare for Divorce

Divorce requires you to be in charge of your money. To get past that fear and to take control, you need to both educate and prepare yourself for your financial independence. This is not an area to tough out on your own or to take risks with your finances. If this frightens you be sure to get the help of a qualified therapist — to overcome any emotional fears around money and the help of a financial adviser to learn about and make informed choices about managing your money. The impact on life is tremendous, which can sometimes make it difficult to know where to begin.

To help get things underway and to start feeling more in control, you might take the following important steps:

Gather your financial records

At some point you will be gathering all of your financial records. Having all the information together and organized will save you time and money. A Divorce Financial Checklist is included in The Smart Divorce® Resource Toolkit, which outlines the key documents that you'll need. If you are in a high conflict situation, or there are trust issues, talk to your lawyer about strategies for gathering your information. Please bear in mind that not everyone will need every document listed. Do not keep these records in your home. Bring copies to your parents, a trusted friend and/or keep them in a safe deposit box that your spouse doesn't know about or have access to.

Open a Post Office Box or other address

This will ensure that you are able to receive confidential mail from your divorce professionals as well as your new credit card and bank statements.

Open a new checking account

Set up a new checking account at a different bank than all other joint accounts. Your divorce lawyer may instruct you to withdraw up to half of your joint funds (state law will dictate what you can and cannot do) and you'll need to put those funds in your new account.

Open new credit cards in your name only

Having a credit card in your name will help you establish your own credit. Also, credit cards may help with day-to-day living expenses during the divorce when some of your other funds may be frozen or unavailable. Do this before any divorce proceedings start, especially if you are not working or if your income is substantially less than your spouse's (you may not be able to get sufficient credit based on your own income).

Get a copy of your credit report

You should immediately get copies of your credit report. You want to be able to resolve any disputes as soon as possible. If you are concerned that your soon-to-be ex-spouse might borrow money in your name, you might want to sign up for a credit monitoring service. These services will notify you anytime there's a change to your credit history. If you have any concerns you should always check with your lawyer, and financial advisor about how you might be affected.

Change your Will and medical directives/living will

You may not want your soon-to-be ex-spouse making medical decisions on your behalf. Further, you most probably won't want your soon to be former spouse to inherit your assets should you die before your divorce is final. Most states will not allow you to totally disinherit your spouse until after the divorce. Check with your lawyer about the prospect of incorporating an Elective Share while you are working through your separation agreement. An Elective Share will give your spouse some percentage of your estate even if you remove your spouse from your will. You will need to redo your Will again after the divorce, when you can legally remove your spouse completely.

Change beneficiaries on life insurance policies, IRAs, and other relevant policies.

If your spouse is not aware of your plans for divorce, you should contact your insurance or brokerage company to make sure they will not automatically send him or her notifications. You don't want to alert your spouse before you are ready. Many 401K plans will not remove a spouse as beneficiary without their written consent.

Take an inventory of all personal (non-marital) property

Consider taking an inventory of all of your personal property. In most states, property that was yours before the marriage is considered to be separate property and most likely will remain yours (there are exceptions to this, such as if you commingled pre-marital funds with marital funds, check with you lawyer for further clarification).

Separate property includes:

- Property that you owned prior to the marriage;
- An inheritance received solely by you;
- A gift you received solely from a third party (your mother gave you her diamond ring).
- The pain and suffering portion of a personal injury judgment;
- Your engagement ring. (This is separate property since you received it before your marriage. However, your wedding band is marital property since it was a gift from your husband during your marriage.)

In general, any gifts that you and your spouse gave each other during the marriage are considered Marital Property. Unfortunately, things often disappear once the divorce process start, so take digital photographs and/or videos of everything and be sure to include a date stamp.

Once you are able to complete many of these important steps, you will not only feel in control, but empowered as well, and in a much stronger emotionally to deal with your divorce.

Financial information and guidance provided by Jeffrey A. Landers.
You may contact Jeffrey by email at landers@bedrockdivorce.com

Jeffrey A. Landers, CDFA is a Divorce Financial Strategist™ and the founder of Bedrock Divorce Advisors, LLC (http://www.BedrockDivorce.com), a divorce financial strategy firm that exclusively works with women, who are going through, or might be going through, a financially complicated divorce. He also advises women business owners on what steps they can take now to "divorce-proof" their business in the event of a future divorce.

How To Tell Your Children You're Divorcing

Research indicates that too few parents sit down and explain to their children that their marriage is ending. They also don't encourage their children to ask questions. Parents often say nothing, leaving their children confused. When parents do not explain what's happening, the children feel anxious, upset and lonely and find it much harder to cope. Children don't need to know the reasons behind the divorce, but what you can tell them is what it means to them and their lives.

Providing age-appropriate information will help your children and adolescents cope with the many changes in their lives initiated by the separation and divorce. It will make them feel less anxious. And it establishes a healthy pattern of communication with your children.

> When parents do not explain what's happening, the children feel anxious, upset and lonely and find it much harder to cope.

Preparing for conversation:

Children and adolescents are much smarter then we often give them credit for. There is information they will want to know and appropriate to share, such as:

The parenting plan.

If you can, try to work out an interim agreement about what your living arrangements will be before you talk with your children. Although this plan might change later, your children will feel more confident if they know you've put some thought into the separation and how it might impact them.

Reassurance

Let your children know that they are equally important to both of you, and you both want to be with them. Assure your children that the divorce is between mom and dad, and not your children -- you will always be their parents.

Answers to their questions

Try to think of the questions that your children might ask and be ready with answers. For example, they will want to know if they will be able to attend the same school or see their friends and extended family and where each of you will be living.

> When it is not possible to talk to children together, do the best that you can to coordinate what you are saying to them and be sure not to put down your co-parent or be negative about them.

Talk about it together

It is helpful for both parents to talk with the children together. This gives them a consistent message and shows them that you both love them and that you can and will work together and parent cooperatively, even though you are divorcing. When it is not possible to talk to children together, do the best that you can to coordinate what you are saying to them and be sure not to put down your co-parent or be negative about them.

Provide the right message

When parents talk to their children about the separation or divorce, they are some very important things that you most likely will want your children to hear:

That it was a mutual decision to separate; avoid laying blame on one parent.

You, their parents, love them very much. and that the divorce is not their fault.

Tell them what their lives will look like in concrete terms. For example: what will stay the same and what may change. Try to provide your children with security and routine.

Allow for grieving:

Don't rush your children; allow them time to react. Children need their space to grieve and adjust to this new reality too. Allow your children to express any and all feelings; let them know that is OK to do so. Also, help your children articulate different feelings and let them know that they can ask you anything.

Help your child understand the new reality:

What will your children's new reality look like? Hang a family calendar in a prominent place or in your children's rooms. Show your children that you care; help them keep track of when they will be in each home. Since they will be adjusting to life in two separate homes, you want them to feel comfortable in this new routine.

And lastly, don't be afraid to tell your children that you, the parents, may not have all the answers, but you are working toward goals together.

13

Smart Co-Parenting and Putting Your Children's Best Interest First

How a Parenting Plan Can Help Structure Effective Co-Parenting

You want to make smart decisions for you and your family. Your family is there forever. But how your family is structured is changing – from both parents in the same home, to living in their individual homes. How the children's time is shared between parents is outlined in a parenting plan. The parenting plan is an agreement between divorcing parents that clearly defines child care and access to the children following a separation. The goals of the parenting plan are to encourage the children's relationship with both parents and to protect the children from parental conflict. It can also be used as an intervention tool to help parents disengage from one another. Parents often fear losing control or being controlled, and a specific, structured plan

> You must realize that because you are parenting in separate households, you can't influence or control what goes on in the other parent's home.

> Having an agreed-to parenting plan in place is like having an insurance policy.

can help ease those feelings.

There is no right or wrong parenting plan. The right plan serves the children's best interest, and that both parents endorse it – if that is possible. It provides a comprehensive schedule of each parent's access to the children, co-parenting responsibilities, and role in decision making. How detailed the parenting plan gets depends on the parents relationship between themselves, and each parent's relationship with their children and of course, children's needs. Some parent's who get along so well feel they don't need a parenting plan. That is actually the best time to develop it, when you are getting along. It avoids conflict if and when it comes up, and maximizes compromise.

There are many decisions and considerations which can be incorporated into the parenting plan. Some parents need lots of details, and some don't. I do not want to suggest that you need to cover all of these issues, but this is a good starting point for many co-parents.

On what days are the children in each family home? How are special days like holidays, birthdays, and special events handled?

What happens at transition times - when your children move from one home to the other? The plan can detail where and what time a parent picks up and drops off their children.

Communication – guidelines for how the parents should communicate between each other. For example verbally or in writing (email). This would provide you with some structure and rules, especially if you are in a high conflict situation. The details help minimize conflict.

When parents don't agree on specific issues, the parenting plan can provide the method to resolve the dispute with a process like mediation or arbitration. Or, you may use a parenting specialist called a parenting coordinator who provides parenting consultation and coaching, and has a limited amount of power to modify the agreement and make decisions when there is an impasse.

Residential schedule - where will the children reside; and how much time will children have with each parent. Also, where will children be picked up and dropped off.

Clothing – who will be responsible for clothing the children?

First Right of Refusal - guidelines for who will provide care for the children when the parent who is responsible for the children at that time, is unable to do so.

School Holidays other Holidays and Vacations – think about what days are important to you and discuss how these times can be shared. The holidays, days off and other important dates to consider are: Easter, Thanksgiving, Passover, Kwanzaa, Christmas, other major religious holidays, New Year's Eve, long weekends, professional development days, birthdays (yours and your children's), Halloween and so on.

Summer Schedule and Holidays – will there be an alternate schedule during this time to include camp, cottages, vacations, etc; or will the children continue with the regular schedule?

Extra-Curricular Activities – how do the children get signed up for programs, how are decisions made, what if the activity falls on the other parent's time, and who ensures the child gets to the activity?

Travel – is each parent allowed to travel with the children outside of the province or state? Is there flexibility if the travel required is on the other parent's time? Note: A Consent to Travel letter needs to be provided when you are traveling alone with your children. This letter needs to be signed by your children's other parent. Templates for a letter may be found online by inputting "consent to travel with one parent" or you may ask your lawyer.

Medical – Who has responsibility for major medical decisions or everyday medical decisions? How do parents communicate with each other about medical issues and outcomes? Who will take the children to the annual check-ups, and what happens in case of an emergency?

Counseling – who has responsibility for making decisions regarding counseling for the children – is this a joint or sole decision?

Education – who has responsibility for choosing which school the children attend – is this joint or sole decision? Do you attend parent interviews together, or on your own? What about other school related decisions such as helping with homework and attending events?

Religion - how are religious differences handled and how are decisions made? Is this a joint or sole decision?

Children's Documents – who has responsibility for them?

Dispute Resolution – in the event that there is a disagreement on a specific issue, protocol can be identified such as using a parenting coordinator or arbitrator.

An opportunity to review the plan is usually built into the initial parenting plan to accommodate changing circumstances. Even when divorcing parents get along well and are flexible about the child-sharing arrangements, having an agreed-to parenting plan in place is like having an insurance policy – it is a fallback plan that you can go to if parental cooperation breaks down and conflict emerges.

There are many resources online to help you come up with ideas for a parenting plan. You might consider working with a parenting expert to help guide you in developing a parenting plan. Your lawyer can also recommend an experienced professional to help develop the plan.

Decision Making and Time Sharing

It is important to understand the difference between the terms custody and access. Access or parenting time, is about time sharing and where the children reside. In legal terms, who has authority to make decisions is referred to as legal custody or decision making. Examples of major decisions include: where the child will go to school, the type of education, religious upbringing, and non-emergency medical decisions. Joint legal custody means that both parents retain legal decision-making authority; they make the decisions together. If one parent has the authority to make decisions it is called sole legal custody. If decision making is a concern for you, then you should speak to your lawyer about this. There are many different permutations to the time sharing or parenting time and it doesn't have to be equal, nor is there one "right" plan. Many co-parents strive to develop a plan that best meets their children's best interest.

Joint Legal Custody - Decision Making

In joint legal custody, both parents retain legal decision-making authority; they make the decisions together. While many separating families are able to co-parent effectively post separation, there are co-parents that might need help if they reach an impasse and can't agree as to what is in the children's best interest. If parents with joint custody have a problem coming to a decision about the child's best interests, this can be resolved by a parenting expert such as an arbitrator or parenting coordinator.

Sole or Full Legal Custody

In sole or full legal custody, only one parent is given decision-making authority over the children, usually because it would be too difficult for the parents to make these decisions together. Needless to say, if you have sole custody, you must be especially careful to act in the best interests of your children. Usually, but not always, the decision-making parent is obligated to keep the other parent informed about the decisions made regarding the children.

Access or Visitation

Time with your children, access or visitation, is often referred to as physical custody – which is defined as to where the children live the majority of the time.

Joint Physical Custody - Parenting Time

In shared or joint custody, the children will have two residences, but the time they spend in each home does not have to be equal. Parenting time can be i) shared parenting time or ii) one parent has primary residence, while the other has other time. If there is one parent with whom the children live with most of the time, this is the custodial or primary parent. The custodial parent is the term that is used for the parent that has primary physical custody of the child. Generally, a custodial parent is also considered a primary care parent. Typically the child resides with the custodial parent. The term non-custodial parent refers to the parent that has the child for a lesser amount of time. Usually, the custodial parent shares joint legal custody with the non-custodial parent, meaning that the custodial parent must inform and consult with the non-custodial parent about the child's education, health care, and other concerns. Typically the child does not reside with the non-custodial parent except during the time that the non-custodial parent exercises his/her visitation right with the child.

Sole Physical Custody

In sole physical custody, the child will live with that parent and may visit the other parent. A parent who has sole physical custody of the children is given full parenting responsibility.

Parenting apart can be complicated and challenging. You must realize that because you are parenting in separate households, you can't influence or control what goes on in the other parent's home.

You want to make smart decisions for your family. Your family is being reconfigured – your children still have two parents but now they live in two separate homes. Parents have both rights and responsibilities concerning their children. They must make decisions regarding their children's health, education, and religion, support their children financially, and provide their children with a home. During the divorce process, the terms used to describe these rights and responsibilities can get confusing. As a result, parental expectations can become unclear. If you have any doubts or concerns, make sure you speak with a family law lawyer.

14

Cooperative Parenting or Parallel Parenting?

Research on families of divorce suggest that there are primarily three styles of parenting for families after a divorce: cooperative, conflicted, or disengaged. Cooperative parenting is the style used by families in which conflict is low and parents can effectively communicate about their child. If you determine that your level of conflict is low, you and the other parent will probably be able to talk about your child's needs in a healthy way. You will probably agree on most parenting values, be relatively consistent in your parenting styles, and have few arguments about your child's life. You will rarely put your child in the middle, and you will solve differences peacefully. Research shows that children of divorce fare best when parents can be cooperative in their parenting. If you fall in this category, you should feel good about yourselves and know that you are helping your child immensely. There are many good books on cooperative parenting designed to help parents do a more effective job.

This Smart Guide focuses on those parents who are in conflict and argue a lot or need to disengage in their parenting.

Even if you can sometimes parent cooperatively, you find it to be difficult and are in conflict too much of the time. Conflicted parenting is the worst for children, who are often in the middle of the conflicts. Your children will adjust to your divorce easier if you can avoid conflicted parenting. Psychological issues that lead to conflicted parenting are many, and may include:

- continuation of hostility that began during the marriage
- differing perceptions of pre-separation child-rearing roles
- differing perceptions of post-separation child-rearing roles
- differing perceptions of how to parent
- concern about the adequacy of the other parent's parenting ability
- an unwillingness of one or both parents to accept the end of the relationship
- jealousy about a new partner in the other parent's life
- contested child custody issues
- personality factors in one or both parents that stimulate conflict.

Whatever the specific source, parents' inability to separate their parental roles from prior conflict in the marriage is often a significant contribution to the conflict after the divorce. This conflict is perhaps the most important variable in determining how your child adjusts to your divorce. Do whatever it takes to change your level of conflict. The first step in this process is to learn to disengage from the other parent. Disengagement is one of the possible styles of parenting after divorce. If you disengage, it's like you have developed a "demilitarized zone" around your children and have little or no contact with the other parent. When you disengage, you will avoid contact with the other parent so that conflict cannot develop. You must do this first to reduce the conflict and before you can move on to the next style of parenting.

> Do whatever it takes to change your level of conflict. The first step in this process is to learn to disengage from the other parent.

The second step in this process is what I call parallel parenting. In this style of parenting, both of you will each learn to parent your child effectively, doing the best job each of you can do during the time you are with your child. You will continue to disengage from the other parent so that conflicts are avoided. If you determine that you cannot cooperatively parent because your level of conflict is moderate or high, disengagement and parallel parenting is the necessary style of parenting.

Parallel parenting gets its name from a similar concept in children's play. Research psychologists have observed that young children who play together, but do not have the skills to interact, engage in a process of parallel play. If they are in a sandbox together or taking turns going down a slide, they play next to one another, not with one another. Each child is doing her own thing with the toys, and generally ignoring the other. When they get older, they will learn to interact cooperatively and play together.

Similarly, parallel parenting is a process of parenting next to one another because you are unable to parent together. Before you can learn to co-parent, you will each learn to parent on your own. The first step of parallel parenting is disengagement. This means that you will not communicate about minor things regarding your child. You will not bicker over things that have always led to conflicts in the past. You will give the other

parent important information about your child, but you will not get into debates about the parenting plan or about each other's parenting style.

"Important information" means the health, welfare, and interests of your child. If your child is sick, you will inform the other parent of this fact, with details on what medication is needed, what has already been administered, and when the next dose is to be given. If your child has a school field trip, you will inform the other parent of the details, and use your parenting plan to decide who might go with the child on the field trip. Each of you should develop independent relationships with your child's teachers, doctors, coaches, and friends so that you don't have to rely on the other parent for your information. Each of you should take turns taking your child to the doctor and dentist. If you are the parent who receives your child's report card, copy it and send it to the other parent. Do this with medical and extra-curricular activity information, such as your child's little league schedule. Do not complain to the other parent when she is ten minutes late for an exchange of your child, and don't argue over whose turn it is to get your child's next haircut. Have parameters in your parenting plan for some of these things and ignore the rest.

When parents are trying to disengage, but communication is necessary, it is often best if non-emergency communication is done by mail, fax or e-mail. Only use faxes if both of you have sufficient privacy where you will receive the fax. By putting your communication in writing, you will have time to gather your thoughts and make sure that the tone is not argumentative. This also lets the receiving parent take some time and gather his thoughts so that he is not impulsive or angry in his response. Sarcasm is never helpful when trying to disengage from conflicts. Don't share your e-mails and faxes with your children; they are simply meant to share important information between the parents. Try to limit non- emergency communication to twice a month, except for sharing information that is time- sensitive

> Accept that there is more than one "right way" to parent. Learn to be less rigid and more accepting of your child's other parent.

(like faxing a notice from school to the other parent on the day you receive it). Obviously, emergency information about illnesses and injuries, unforeseen delays in visitation (as a result of traffic conditions, for example), or immediate school concerns should be shared by phone as soon as possible. However, by reducing general communication, and by putting necessary communications in writing, you will go a long way toward disengaging from conflict.

If you have very young children, you know it is important to share all aspects of your child's functions with the care provider when you drop her off. In the same way, it is critical for parents to share detailed information with each other upon the exchange of the child. A useful tool is a "parent communication notebook." In this notebook you will write down the highlights of your child's emotions and behaviors during the time she's with you. Fill out the notebook in great detail and pass it along to the other parent at the time of transition. Things to include in this notebook are your observations of your child's health, feeding and sleeping patterns, language issues, your child's mood, what soothes your child, what upsets your child, your daily routine, and any other detailed information about your child's functions and needs. This notebook should stay

with your child so both parents can use it as a forum for preserving thoughts about your child and her needs.

Another step in parallel parenting is not telling the other

parent how to parent, and ignoring (rather than arguing back) when the other parent tries to tell you how to parent. Support different styles of parenting in order to avoid conflict. Obviously, some things are very important, such as consistent discipline philosophies and techniques, adequate supervision, giving your child necessary medication, and ensuring that your child gets to school on time with homework completed. If you have concerns about these very important issues, you will need a forum for working out your differences.

There are many things that parents argue about that aren't so important. Some of this is related to different parenting philosophies and some of it is related to the difficulty of sharing your child. Accept that there is more than one "right way" to parent. Learn to be less rigid and more accepting of your child's other parent. Rather than trying to change how the other parent does his job of parenting, do your best job of parenting during the time your child is with you, without criticizing the other parent. Children are capable of being parented in two different styles, and many children of divorce adjust quite well to two very different homes. Remember, just as you will want to avoid criticizing the other parent, you will not want to deal with criticism of your parenting techniques.

Excerpted from Chapter 2 of *Parenting After Divorce, 2nd Edition* (Impact Publishers, 2008). © Philip M. Stahl, Ph.D.

Information and guidance provided by Phil Stahl, Ph.D., You may contact Dr. Stahl by e-mail at philipstahlphd@gmail.com

Dr. Stahl is a licensed psychologist, practitioner, teacher, and author, specializing in high conflict families of divorce. He has served on numerous committees and task forces designed to improve the quality of work in his field. In addition, Dr. Stahl teaches judges, attorneys, psychologists and other mental health professionals about issues affecting families and children.

15

Living Separate and Apart

In most jurisdictions the reasons contributing to the breakdown of a marriage don't matter – this is called "no fault" divorce. This means, the grounds on which to base a claim for divorce is simply marriage breakdown. In most instances, in the legal arena, the reasons behind the divorce decision don't matter. One way to establish that a marriage has broken down is to show that the spouses have lived separate and apart; in many jurisdictions this period is at least one year, this is relevant only to get a divorce. Please check with your legal counsel to confirm the legal requirements.

The day you officially decide to live separate and apart, is important as it will determine your date of separation, and the date upon which your assets are valued. This date is usually referred to as valuation date or date of separation.

Generally speaking, the courts have held that "separate and apart" means a physical separation, combined with an intent to end the marriage. This intent does not need to be shared by both parties. In some situations, spouses can be considered to have been living separate and apart while continuing to live under the same roof, but no longer living like husband and wife.

In most instances when a couple separates, one of the partners' usually moves out of the matrimonial home, also called the family residence. However, this isn't always the case as it may not be financially feasible, some are afraid it will put them on an unequal legal footing, or one of the parties for what ever reason, does not wish to move out during the separation. Whether you choose to stay, or move out of the matrimonial home, ask your legal counsel if there are any consequences for leaving the family residence. Too often people are misinformed about what, if any repercussions are for moving or staying, so it's always best to ask your lawyer this question.

> Your behavior now could have long term consequences in terms of your family relationships and finances.

Even when a divorce is amicable, there may be usually some significant emotional strain, stress and tension if both parties remain under the same roof. Seeing the person everyday that you are divorcing could cause anger, jealousy and other emotions or manifest itself in other ways such as affecting your eating or sleeping patterns, and so forth.

There are alternatives to living under the same roof that could be considered, such as: moving in with parents, siblings and friends, or renting a room versus an apartment. However, before you do anything, this should be discussed with your lawyer. Nevertheless, if for various reasons alternatives are not possible here are some tips to minimize the stress and tension while working through the separation.

Living Separate and Apart: Together in the Matrimonial/Family Home

Coping with your soon to be former spouse

Give each other space. Try to keep your dating and new social life out of the picture. If one of you has a new partner, try to keep that information private, and avoid bringing your new partner home.

Avoid sharing a room or a bed with your children. Sleeping with your child might set up bad sleeping behaviors that will be difficult to change once you move out of their bedroom.

Accept responsibility for your own life chores. Don't expect your soon to be former partner to be doing the little things for you that he or she once did, for example: taking your laundry to the cleaners, or on a grander scale doing your laundry or cooking. You might consider developing a cleaning schedule.

Seek to begin your independent life. The everyday tasks you shared as a couple could now be assumed by the individual responsible. For example: schedule your own appointments.

Discuss the finances of living together. A discussion about how the bills are going to be paid could help determine some ground rules and clarity, for example: is one of you going to accept full responsibility for all expenses, are the expenses factored into the financial negotiations and so on. Another important consideration to is how the mortgage is to be handled. This may be a legal issue, and should be discussed with your lawyer.

Be civil. There will be an end to this difficult situation. Try to be respectful.

Helping Your Children Cope While Living in the Same Home, Separate and Apart

Talk to your children. You might consider letting your children know that you have separated. If you are not sure what to say or do, speak to a parenting expert.

Consider implementing structure and routine. You might implement an interim parenting plan agreement, but once again, make sure you discuss this with your lawyer. The parenting plan is a detailed schedule of how the children's time is to be shared between the parents. If you don't have a plan at this time, provide your children with a sense of security, and let them know how and when you plan on spending time with them and so on. Discuss with your soon to be co-parent how responsibilities are to be shared,

Keep new partners private. Do not expose your children to new love interests. Some therapists suggest that you refrain from introducing your children to a new partner for at least one year, or until you know that this is a serious and lasting relationship.

Don't involve your children in your divorce. Do not discuss the progression of the legal divorce with your children; this is an adult matter and personal. You should not want to affect their relationship with their other parent or burden your children – your divorce is not their business.

Instill important messages: We love you very much, we are still your parents, the divorce is not your fault; and give your children a sense of security.

Living Separate and Apart: Transitioning from Our Home to My Home

The home that you shared as a couple, might now become the exclusive possession of one of you. For many, there are emotional ties, fond memories, and feelings of security around the home. Sometimes, maintaining the family home is emotionally appealing, but financially disastrous. Sometimes it can be kept without creating financial hardship. Talk to your lawyer about what your rights are to help make the process move smoothly. You might also consider speaking to a therapist, family or a trusted friend for emotional support during this potentially difficult time.

Considerations When Moving Out of the Matrimonial Home:

For the Spouse Moving:

Know your budget. Ensure that what ever you decide to rent or buy is within your budget. You don't want to carry a mortgage or pay rent on housing you cannot afford. Divorce is a stressful time, compounding that stress with additional financial pressures may have long term financial and emotional consequences. You can always upgrade once you finalize the separation agreement.

Don't make rash decisions. Carefully consider your next move. You want to turn this new residence into a home, and fresh start.

Closeness counts. If you have children, living nearby will help foster a good co-parenting relationship, and facilitate ongoing contact with your children.

Safety first. If you need to move out for reasons of safety and wellbeing, for you or your children, consult with a family law lawyer to ensure you are making this move effectively and in your best interests.

Reduce the tension and stress. If you have an amicable relationship with your soon to be former partner, discuss the timing for moving your belongings. However, if it's a high conflict situation then you might want to ask your lawyer the parameters around when you or your spouse can take their things, and what items are allowed to be removed from the matrimonial home.

Helping your children adjust to a parent moving out

Get them involved. Involving the children in the changes is helpful. If they are going to be moving, and/or getting a new bedroom, let them see the new home or pick out their new furniture. This will provide them with a sense of comfort in their new surroundings.

Make them feel at home. As much as you can, duplicate at your home the little things that your children love at your co-parent's home. For example: Barbie dolls, books, and so on. Send out the message that you care. Duplicating items will remove the stress children may feel about taking their favorite things to the other parent's home or about forgetting to bring them. Keep in mind that some items, such as a favorite blanket or stuffed animal, or high priced items like a laptop, computer, or IPod can't be duplicated.

> Duplicating items will remove the stress children may feel about taking their favorite things to the other parent's home or about forgetting to bring them.

It's the little things that matter too. Ease transition and moving by having all of your children's toiletries available at each residence. For example: teenage girls might want their hair care products, makeup and feminine hygiene products; teenage boys might want their shaving creams and shavers. Younger children might have their favorite brand of toiletries too.

Other Considerations and Questions

Some couples to try to reconcile while living separate and apart. If you tried to reconcile, what ever the outcome, good for you for trying. If you attempt a reconciliation, and live together again for a period of time, but the reconciliation did not work, you will need to discuss this with your lawyer. You will also need to determine whether there was a time lapse significant to start the one year period over again, or whether the timing can be considered uninterrupted.

There are other considerations which your might be brought forward to family law lawyer. Other items to discuss include:

- Does moving out before the separation agreement affect the financial outcome, and if so, how?
- Does leaving the matrimonial /family home affect how the parenting plan is developed?
- What happens when a spouse who has moved out wants to move back in?
- Can the locks be changed once a spouse has moved out?
- What if neither spouse wants to leave the matrimonial home? Can I force my spouse to leave?
- When can I sell the matrimonial home if my spouse has moved out?
- If a pre-nuptial agreement was signed, and an agreement was made that the home belongs to my spouse, can I be forced to leave before the separation agreement is finalized?
- What if a pre-nuptial agreement was signed and an agreement was made that the home belongs to me, can I ask my spouse to leave? If so, how much notice needs to be provided?
- If my spouse has left the family home is he or she entitled to a key?
- If my spouse has left the family home how is it arranged for him or her to take their belongings, or other items?
- What if my spouse has moved out and we haven't agreed how to divide up furniture and other items, how is ownership determined?
- If my spouse has moved out of the home, can I sell the home without

his/her permission?
- What if my spouse has locked me out and won't let me back in to retrieve my belongings?
- Can my spouse move back in if we are living separate and apart?
- Who is responsible for the bills on the house while living separate and apart?
- Who is responsible for repairs on the house while living separate and apart?
- What do I do if my spouse is not honoring his/her financial obligations while we are living separate and apart?

Moving out of the matrimonial home is not uncommon prior to divorce, but not compulsory. Meeting the requirements for living separate and apart is a legal requirement that doesn't necessarily have to be done by moving out. However, laws and requirement differ by jurisdiction, so it is important to discuss this matter with a family law lawyer.

Being aware of your rights and responsibilities cannot be overlooked when taking into consideration your costs of living separate and apart; try not to do anything that might negatively affect your relationship with your soon to be former spouse (especially when negotiating your separation agreement), or impact your relationship with your children. You want to carefully think through how you begin the process of living separate and apart, as your behavior now could have long term consequences in terms of your family relationships and finances.

Smart Co-Parenting for the New Family Unit

While parents are likely to approach remarriage or repartnering and a new blended family with great happiness and joy, your children or your new spouse's children may feel left out of your choice to blend, and uncertain about this new family unit. The children might have questions like: What will the new person in their life mean to them? What will their new step-siblings be like? How will their relationship with their biological parents change?

As you get ready to join your families, a few important things to remember are:

- Be realistic: things won't be perfect overnight.

- Be patient: good relationships take time and children need to time to trust and count on you.

- Limit your expectations: know that you will probably give a lot of time, energy, love and affection to this new family relationship that my not be returned the same way by all of the children. Your children, or your new partner's children, might not feel the same way you do, yet. Building relationships take time. Don't expect everyone to feel they have to be as enthusiastic as you are at the beginning. Give the relationship time to feel comfortable; and for the love affection to build.

Tips for successfully blending families

Help the children adapt to the new family configuration. Children will belong to two households and families; they will need guidance and time to adjust to different set of rules, expectations, and systems.

Bonding takes time. Don't expect children to love and adore each other, or your new partner right away. In some cases, the best case scenario would be working towards courtesy and respect. Building caring relationships between children and their new step-parent and step family is a process that requires time and patience.

Be open to discussion. Creating opportunities for family discussions, problem-solving and negotiation helps children better manage and cope with this new family structure. Prepare the family for a change. Establishing new family patterns, rituals and traditions help children feel a sense of belonging and shared memories.

Understand the new relationship. Clarifying roles, responsibilities and expectations in the blended family serves as a "road map" with strategies for building relationships and a solid framework for the family unit.

Develop a conflict resolution strategy. Conflict is a part of all families. Combined families have more complex and diverse needs and emotions in dealing with conflict; a solid conflict resolution model helps to address these issues.

Demonstrate your love. Children need reassurance that they are loved and are still a priority to their biological parent, as loyalty issues can arise.

Discipline your own, and step back for his/her children. The general rule of thumb about discipline is that the biological parent is the one who guides the discipline for their own children when there are step-children living together. However, you might consider and discuss with the new step parent household rules. Some things to think about include: rules, discipline, curfews, allowances and so on. If there are differences between each family as you merge into one, then you might have a family meeting, or discuss the issues privately with the children so they understand the differences, you want to try to avoid resentment. Further, ensure open discussion with your partner about any of this to ensure open communication, understanding, and support.

How to Tell Your Spouse You Want a Divorce

Talking to your partner about divorce may be one of the most difficult conversations you will ever have with him or her. Deciding to marry was probably a conversation of mutual happiness and agreement. However, the discussion surrounding divorce is in most cases, not something you are both in agreement. If you've discussed divorce in the past, then news of your decision might be met with less surprise, in other instances, your partner may be blindsided. Some partners feel blindsided even when the issues has been discussed. This is likely going to be a very difficult conversation, but one you cannot avoid.

In most instances, the news will hurt, and can be very emotional. Your partner may be in denial, and try to hurt you back. The way you separate will dictate the course of the separation, and whether it will be amicable or not (for some, not all).

Preparing for the conversation

Try to foresee how you think your partner will react, and have a friend or family member on alter to the event. You don't need to tell them what is going on, but you might say "I think that (my partner) may need you in the next couple of days.

Separate with your spouse's dignity intact. Try to determine how your current actions will impact your relationship in the future. In many cases the leaving partner has been thinking about the decision for quite some time while the left behind spouse is just coming to terms with the decision. Consider how your actions to move on in your life before and following the announcement may make the left partner feel.

> Separate with your spouse's dignity intact. Try to determine how your current actions will impact your relationship in the future.

Have the conversation in a safe neutral environment. You don't want to tell them in a public place where they might be embarrassed from an emotional breakdown, and you don't want to tell your spouse when the kids are at home.

If you're anticipating that the reaction may be so negative that the person may become abusive, ensure you have made arrangements for your safety.

Speak with kindness

You want to tell your spouse in a kind way that you want a divorce, be sure to begin with the things that you have loved and appreciated over the years.

When you've grown apart - you might say: You both see things differently now. It's fair to recognize, that you both have changed. I've been tending to the needs of the family and the household and I want to tend to my needs now. Either partner, or both, feels as though they may have been sacrificing for others throughout their whole adult life and not have had the opportunity to think about their own needs.

Acknowledge their accomplishments

Talk about what you have done together, raised children and so on.

Talk about the contributions he or she has made to the relationship and family regarding finances, friendships and the like.

DO:
- Allow your partner to save face. Don't tell him/her you are leaving

because you just don't love them or they aren't meeting your needs; talk about what you want to do in your life instead. For example, what you need or want for your life as opposed to what they didn't give you.

- Recognize it's a loss for both of you. The leaving partner should be empathic to their partner, but understand that their spouse is not likely to understand that you might be grieving too.
- Cry together. Regardless of who initiates, see it as a grieving process for you both
- Acknowledge that the leaving partner has had more time to grieve the decision and offer time to get to the same place.
- Go for separation counseling. This will help you communicate more effectively and with dignity, honesty and respect.
- Develop a phase out plan, phase out with agreement.
- Count on behaviour that you may not have anticipated and be proactive. So have an understanding before you go into this, irrespective of how amicable you are that in these situations, people behave in ways that wouldn't have otherwise been anticipated.

DON'T

- Don't rewrite history and tell your spouse your reason for divorcing that will make you feel better.
- Don't flout a relationship that you may have on the side, don't humiliate your partner unnecessarily.

> You want to tell your spouse in a kind way that you want a divorce, be sure to begin with the things that you have loved and appreciated over the years.

- Don't have a process server serve your partner before you have told him or her of your decision (if possible.) Tell your partner yourself, and you may want to say, I'm going to be seeing a lawyer.
- Don't say my lawyer is going to be in touch with you tomorrow, and you're going to be paying dearly. What you want to say instead is: how do you want to do this, and be armed with the information to share.

- Don't announce it to everyone until you are in agreement.

Phase out with agreement

- If you're living together in the matrimonial home, think about when to move out of the bedroom, bathroom, making appointments, social engagements and so on. Be kind, talk about how it should look. For example, tell your partner: You need to make your own doctor appointments now; we planned to go away on a holiday what do you want to do about that now.
- Begin to phase out of previous roles and obligations, such as scheduling appointments, social engagements
- Begin to take on new roles such as taking out the garbage or scheduling your own appointments. Start to be more independent
- If you can legally do so, begin to separate finances by opening your own account paying the bills you were typically responsible from your own account. Apply for your own credit card.....start your own independence. (always check with legal counsel before you do anything)
- Set your own schedule as to when you work and when you go out, but it is a courtesy to let someone know when you will be back.
- Try to work on opposite shifts, go out after work and/or leave for work earlier.

> Most important is to show compassion and empathy. While this conversation may hurt someone's feelings, you don't want to deliberately hurt their feelings. The goal should be, if you're able, to pave the way for an ongoing relationship.

What do to when one spouse doesn't want to separate

When someone is very resistant, you may want to involve a neutral family friend, clergy or therapist.

Recognize that it may take some time to accept and process, don't expect your spouse to accept it the next day. Just because someone is resistant it isn't unusual.

See a therapist together – while your spouse may go because she/he thinks it may give them the opportunity to reconcile, they may be able to hear from someone else that there isn't a possibility of reconciliation. They may also gain a rapport and be willing to return individually.

Go to separation counseling. If your spouse is being resistant, a counselor can help you with the best way to tell your children, and how to better communicate during this time.

Planning the divorce conversation when there are children

Set up a parenting schedule in the same house or move to a nesting situation. Nesting: when parents go in and out of the house, or one parent lives in the basement and the other parent lives upstairs. Some parents both remain in the same living quarters but one parent has parenting time and is responsible for the children while the other remains in a more private space of the home. This arrangement is only appropriate when both parents are amicable and can put the needs of the children first.

If you're a stay at home parent, then schedule times that the other parent will have parenting responsibility.

If the children are seeing the conflict do what you can to separate within the house, move out of bedroom and the like. If after giving time and opportunity to talk to supportive friend and therapist, and your spouse is still resistant, your children likely aware of conflict and one parent may need to tell them. Don't do so until you tell spouse when you intend to do it and ask him or her to join you.

When is it appropriate to tell your children you're divorcing without the other parent present?

Sometimes a parent may have to tell the children on their own. If you've already given your partner significant time to accept the reality, and they are refusing to speak to the children, you may have to tell them on your own. Note: It's only fair to give your spouse some time, you can't expect them to come to terms with it right away. Tell your spouse that you are going to do this, and give them the opportunity to join you.

If it's just you talking to your children. You have to tell them you've made the decision and that the other parent isn't accepting it well, that you are doing all that you can to support him/her and that you're doing everything you can to support them.

However, you felt that you the child needed to know, because there will be changes in the house. And then tell them what the changes will be. There is nothing worse than everyone knowing but the children, and the children knowing that everyone knows except for them – like the worst kept secret.

In most cases, once the parent accepts it, they will be able to put the needs of the children ahead of their own.

Most important is to show compassion and empathy. While this conversation may hurt someone's feelings, you don't want to deliberately hurt their feelings. The goal should be, if you're able, to pave the way for an ongoing relationship. Just keep in mind that your spouse will need some time to process this conversation.

Information and guidance provided by Jacqueline Vanbetlehem, RSW, Acc.F.M.
You may contact Ms. Vanbetlehem by email at jacqueline@vanbetlehem.ca

Jacqueline Vanbetlehem is a social worker and mediator in private practice in Oakville, Ontario.

What to Tell the Kids About a High-Conflict Co-Parent

Many parents have asked us about how to raise a child or children with a co-parent (whether a spouse, former spouse or unmarried partner) who is "high-conflict." In other words, the co-parent frequently exhibits some or all of the following:

- preoccupied with blaming others (often those closest to him/her, like the child or the other parent – or both)
- extreme behaviors (like yelling, hitting spouse or child, making false allegations, spreading rumors, hiding money, and so forth)
- all-or-nothing thinking (solutions to problems have to be all their way; they see some people (including themselves) as all-good and others (including you) as all-bad; may see one of his or her children as all-good and the other as all-bad)
- unmanaged emotions (screaming, crying, pleading) – but some don't show this.

If you are a parent who is asking this question, it is very important to avoid being accused of "bad-mouthing" the other parent, by speaking negatively about him or her to the children and providing too much information about adult issues, such as a court case. On the other hand, you want to protect your children from the blaming and uncontrolled behavior of the high-conflict co-parent, and to provide the children with coping skills and help them not blame themselves.

This article discusses one way parents can deal with both concerns, while helping your children to be resilient throughout their lives.

Teach Four Big Skills

Rather than talking to the kids about the "high-conflict" co-parent (and you should never use that term around the children), talk about "four big skills for life." These skills are:

- flexible thinking
- managed emotions
- moderate behaviors
- checking ourselves to see if we're using these skills regularly

Tell your kids that these are four big skills that will help them with friends, help them get a good job someday, and may help them be community leaders someday, if they want. These four skills help in any relationship, whether it's someone you like or someone you don't like. You can explain this to a child of almost any age, starting at least at age four, if you put it in simple terms.

Then, in daily life you can ask them if they noticed other people who used these skills in solving problems, or if you used any of these four skills in solving a problem. For example: "Did you notice how that guy at the store was frustrated, but he stayed calm and listened to the clerk tell him where to find what he wanted? Would you say he was managing his emotions?"

> It is very important to avoid being accused of "bad-mouthing" the other parent, by speaking negatively about him or her to the children and providing too much information about adult issues, such as a court case.

"Did you notice how that guy on TV was just yelling at a store clerk. Would you say he was managing his emotions? Did he seem to get what he wanted? No, he didn't. How do you think he could have used managed emotions to help solve his problem?"

An example you could share about yourself: "Today I was real frustrated by sitting still in a traffic jam. But I told myself to think about things I was looking forward to this week – like your birthday party, and seeing my sister, and a movie I want to see someday. I used my flexible thinking and managed my emotions. But it wasn't easy. I kept having bad thoughts about the other drivers in front of me, but then I chose my happy thoughts again. Did you have any frustrating times today that you dealt with by using your flexible thinking?"

> Tell your kids that these are four big skills that will help them with friends, help them get a good job someday, and may help them be community leaders someday, if they want.

Help Your Child Cope with Friends

Once you've started to have these casual discussions with your child, you can teach these skills when they have a conflict with a friend. For example: "Mom/Dad, this kid at school says he hates me! I feel like punching him in the nose! He/she used to be my best friend!"

Then, you could say something like: "Oh, that's too bad. I remember when that happened to me. I can understand how angry you must have felt. But I'm glad you didn't punch him/her in the nose. Have you thought of what you can do instead? Maybe you can talk with him/her, after you've both calmed down. Try to use your flexible thinking to come up with ideas of what went wrong and how you can solve it."

You can also do this when conflicts come up between siblings, and especially praise them when they solve their own problems. You could say: "I'm really glad that you both were able to solve this problem on your own. You're pretty good problem-solvers, especially when you use your flexible thinking like you just did." Catch them when they're doing well. (You get more of what you pay attention to.)

Help Your Child Cope with Your Co-Parent

Now, since you have taken an educational approach to teaching these four big skills, you can start using them when things happen with your co-parent. Suppose he or she was unreasonably angry at your child, and the child came to you to complain. Rather than saying that your co-parent is a jerk, you could say: "Remember, some people have a harder time managing their emotions than other people. When you're ready, let's do some flexible thinking about ways you might deal with situations like that in the future. In the meantime, we can manage our own emotions, even though some other people can't."

By speaking in this "teaching skills" way about the other parent, you avoid "bad-mouthing" him or her, while giving your child skills for resilience. This way, you can't be blamed for saying anything specifically about your co-parent. Instead, you have kept it as a general lesson and still provided a discussion about what to do in the future in "situations like that."

By teaching the four big skills for life, your child can learn lessons that will last into adulthood, even during the most difficult times of childhood – including separation and divorce.

Information and guidance provided by Bill Eddy, LCSW, Esq. You may contact Bill Eddy by e-mail at info@highconflictinstitute.com

Bill Eddy is a lawyer, therapist, mediator and the President of High Conflict Institute. He developed the "High Conflict Personality" theory (HCP Theory) and has become an international expert on managing disputes involving high conflict personalities and personality disorders. He provides training on this subject to lawyers, judges, mediators, managers, human resource professionals, businesspersons, healthcare administrators, college administrators, homeowners' association managers, ombudspersons, law enforcement, therapists and others. He has been a speaker and trainer in over 25 states, several provinces in Canada, Australia, France and Sweden.

A B.I.F.F. Response to Hostile Email

BRIEF

Keep your response brief. This will reduce the chances of a prolonged and angry back and forth. The more you write, the more material the other person has to criticize. Keeping it brief signals that you don't wish to get into a dialogue. Just make your response and end your letter. Don't take their statements personally and don't respond with a personal attack. Avoid focusing on comments about the person's character, such as saying he or she is rude, insensitive, or stupid. It just escalates the conflict and keeps it going. You don't have to defend yourself to someone you disagree with. If your friends still like you, you don't have to prove anything to those who don't.

INFORMATIVE

The main reason to respond to hostile mail is to correct inaccurate statements which might be seen by others. "Just the facts" is a good idea. Focus on the accurate statements you want to make, not on the inaccurate statements the other person made. For example: "Just to clear things up, I was out of town on February 12th, so I would not have been the person who was making loud noises that day."

Avoid negative comments. Avoid sarcasm. Avoid threats. Avoid personal remarks about the other's intelligence, ethics or moral behavior. If the other person has a "high conflict personality," you will have no success in reducing the conflict with personal attacks. While most people can ignore personal attacks or might think harder about what you are saying, high conflict people feel they have no choice but to respond in anger – and keep the conflict going. Personal attacks rarely lead to insight or positive change.

FRIENDLY

While you may be tempted to write in anger, you are more likely to achieve your goals by writing in a friendly manner. Consciously thinking about a friendly response will increase your chances of getting a friendly – or neutral – response in return. If your goal is to end the conflict, then being friendly has the greatest likelihood of success. Don't give the other person a reason to get defensive and keep responding.

This does not mean that you have to be overly friendly. Just make it sound a little relaxed and non-antagonistic. If appropriate, say you recognize their concerns. Brief comments that show your empathy and respect will generally calm the other person down, even if only for a short time.

FIRM

In a non-threatening way, clearly tell the other person your information or position on an issue. (For example: "That's all I'm going to say on this issue.") Be careful not to make comments that invite more discussion, unless you are negotiating an issue or want to keep a dialogue going back and forth. Avoid comments that leave an opening, such as: "I hope you will agree with me that ..." This invites the other person to tell you "I don't agree."

Sound confident and don't ask for more information, if you want to end the back-and-forth. A confident-sounding person is less likely to be challenged with further emails. If you get further emails, you can ignore them, if you have already sufficiently addressed the inaccurate information. If you need to respond again, keep it even briefer and do not

Keep your response brief. This will reduce the chances of a prolonged and angry back and forth.

emotionally engage. In fact, it often helps to just repeat the key information using the same words.

Example

Joe's email: "Jane, I can't believe you are so stupid as to think that I'm going to let you take the children to your boss' birthday party during my parenting time. Have you no memory of the last six conflicts we've had about my parenting time? Or are you having an affair with him? I always knew you would do anything to get ahead! In fact, I remember coming to your office party witnessing you making a total fool of yourself – including flirting with everyone from the CEO down to the mailroom kid! Are you high on something? Haven't you gotten your finances together enough to support yourself yet, without flinging yourself at every Tom, Dick and Harry? ..." [And on and on and on.]

> The main reason to respond to hostile mail is to correct inaccurate statements which might be seen by others. "Just the Facts" is a good idea.

Jane's Response: "Thank you for responding to my request to take the children to my office party. Just to clarify, the party will be from 3-5 on Friday at the office and there will be approximately 30 people there – including several other parents bringing school-age children. There will be no alcohol, as it is a family-oriented firm and there will be family-oriented activities. I think it will be a good experience for them to see me at my workplace. Since you do not agree, then of course I will respect that and withdraw my request, as I recognize it is your parenting time." [And that's the end of her email.]

Comment: Jane kept it brief, and did not engage in defending herself. Since this was just between them, she didn't need to respond. If he sent this email to friends, co-workers or family members (which high conflict people often do), then she would need to respond to the larger group with more information, such as the following:

Jane's Group Response: "Dear friends and family: As you know, Joe and I had a difficult divorce. He has sent you a private email showing correspondence between us about a parenting schedule matter. I hope you will see this as a private matter and understand that you do not need to respond or get involved in any way. Almost everything he has said is in anger and not at all accurate. If you have any questions for me personally, please feel free to contact me and I will clarify anything I can. I appreciate your friendship and support."

And that's it: B.I.F.F.!

Whether you are at work, at home or elsewhere, a B.I.F.F. response can save you time and emotional anguish. The more people who handle hostile mail in such a manner, the less hostile mail there will be.

Excerpted from Don't Alienate the Kids! Raising Resilient Children While Avoiding High Conflict Divorce © 2010 by Bill Eddy (High Conflict Institute Press, www.HCIPress.com)

See also: BIFF: Quick Responses to High Conflict People, Their Personal Attacks, Hostile Email and Social Media Meltdowns © 2011 by Bill Eddy (High Conflict Institute Press, www.HCIPress.com)

Information and guidance provided by Bill Eddy, LCSW, Esq. You may contact Bill Eddy by e-mail at info@highconflictinstitute.com

Bill Eddy is a lawyer, therapist, mediator and the President of High Conflict Institute. He developed the "High Conflict Personality" theory (HCP Theory) and has become an international expert on managing disputes involving high conflict personalities and personality disorders. He provides training on this subject to lawyers, judges, mediators, managers, human resource professionals, businesspersons, healthcare administrators, college administrators, homeowners' association managers, ombudspersons, law enforcement, therapists and others. He has been a speaker and trainer in over 25 states, several provinces in Canada, Australia, France and Sweden.

SEPARATING SAFELY

Knowing the risks of abuse following separation and divorce for you and your children.

Are you at risk?

Research demonstrates that the risk of lethal violence is particularly high in the first few months following separation (Campbell, Glass, Sharps, Laughon, & Bloom, 2007). In addition to an elevated risk of lethal violence, there is also an increased risk for non-lethal violence post-separation. Evidence suggests that those who are physically violent against their partner before a separation will often become psychologically violent following separation (Brownridge, 2006). Thirty percent of divorced or separated men had perpetrated acts of violence against their partners in a national sample of 1834 Canadians, in comparison to only eighteen percent of their married counterparts (Lupri, 1990).

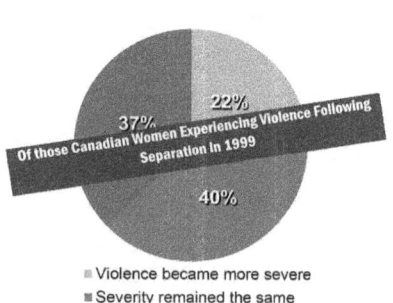

Of those Canadian Women Experiencing Violence Following Separation in 1999
- 22%
- 37%
- 40%
- Violence became more severe
- Severity remained the same
- Violence began after separation

What about your children?

Following divorce, violent partners have been shown to use access with children or legal custody proceedings to control their former partners (Radford et al., 1997; Harrison, 2008). Watson and Ancis (2013) found that in couples where abuse was a factor in their married or former relationship, during divorce proceedings, child support litigation, custody and visitation battles, and prolonging the case were used against abuse victims as a way for perpetrators to exert power and control over their former spouses even in divorce.

This control is not only exerted over the parent, but also the children, as the abusive parent often threaten to take the children away or use the children as weapons against the other parent by undermining the non-abusive parent's credibility and telling the children the separation is their fault (Van Horn & McAlister Groves, 2006).

Are you being abusive?

If you are abusing your former partner, you first need to accept that you have a problem that requires help. No form of abuse is acceptable, and while some may seem more serious than others, they can escalate and all need to be addressed. Once you have accepted that there is a problem, you have already become part of the solution. You need to know that help is available to you, the following agencies will direct you to the best place to get it.

"I've left the relationship, I'm safe now…"

Not necessarily. Domestic violence is often considered an individual's attempt at gaining and maintaining control. When separation or divorce occurs, regardless of whether a partner was or was not abusive during a relationship, they may become abusive as a means to gain the control they feel that they have lost. These individuals may try to regain this control through various measures.

You need to identify your former partner's use and level of force so that you can assess the risk of danger to you and your children before it occurs. See the below means of power and control used by abusive partners following separation and divorce to assess your risk.

Harassment

Your former partner or spouse...
- Hangs around your neighbourhood
- Tries to contact you by phone, letter, e-mail, fax, graffiti or by putting notes on your car
- Calls your home or your family repeatedly to trace you
- Forces their way into your home, saying they are entitled because they are your partner
- Harasses you by legal means - for instance, makes false allegations about you to child protective services or files repeated family law claims

> Partner Assault Response (PAR) programs, a component of Ontario's Domestic Violence Court program, are specialized counselling and educational services offered by community-based agencies to people who have assaulted their partners. While an offender is in the PAR program, staff offer their partner help with safety planning, referrals to community resources, and information about the offender's progress. To find the PAR office nearest you, call the Victim Support Line toll-free at 1-888-579-2888, or 416-314-2447 in the Greater Toronto Area.

Psychological

Your former partner or spouse...
- Makes you feel guilty and inadequate with the things they say
- Criticizes what you do and how you do it
- Threatens to kidnap your children if you do not comply with what they want
- Threatens to take custody away from you or prevent you from obtaining custody
- Threatens to harm you physically

- Makes suicide threats
- Threatens to kill you or your children

Sexual
- Demands that you have sex with him or her
- Interrogates you about your sex life
- Force his or her way into your home and rapes you (or sexually assaults you)

Verbal Abuse
- Raises his or her voice with you
- Yells at you
- Swears at you

Financial
- Limits your financial means (i.e, cancels credit cards, bank accounts, etc.)
- Increases debt (i.e., maxing out credit cards, making extravagant purchases on joint accounts)
- Limits your health benefits, insurance, etc.

What do I do?

should:
- Open a savings account in your name to *increase your independence*
- Exchange the children in a **public place** - if this is impossible, exchange the children outside the home (i.e., on the sidewalk, for instance)
- **Shorten the time** it takes to hand over the children by making sure everything is ready when your former partner is scheduled to pick them up
- **Minimize communication** with your former partner as much as possible. You can do this by, writing any necessary information regarding the children in a diary kept in one of the children's bag, communicating via e-mail rather than phone.
- **Stay Safe** by filing a police complaint and note down fact that can constitute solid evidence in a complaint filed with the police (i.e., threats, physical or sexual abuse of the children or yourself, alcohol or drug abuse)
- **Have your lawyer request** that certain terms and conditions be include in

the court ruling (i.e., who is entitled to have contact with the children, neither parent saying negative things to the children about the other parent, measures to ensure there are no restrictions on communication with the children, clearly delineate property division, place and conditions for child exchange, etc.)

Bryanne Harris, M.A. (Counselling Psychology). You may contact Ms. Harris by e-mail atbharri33@uwo.ca

Bryanne Harris is a Psychologist (Cand. Reg.) specializing in high-conflict divorce and court-ordered assessments. She recently received her Master of Arts in Counselling Psychology from the University of Western Ontario in London, Ontario and completed her Master's Thesis on gender bias in parental alienation in the Canadian court system. Ms. Harris has also conducted research on domestic violence, divorce, and teacher sexual misconduct, among other topics.

Resources

Brownridge, D.A. (2006). Violence against women post-separation. *Aggression and Violent Behavior*, 11, 514-530.

Campbell, J.C., Glass, N., Sharps, P.W., Laughon, K., & Bloom, T. (2007). Intimate partner homicide: Review and implications of research and policy. *Trauma, Violence & Abuse*, 8, 246-269.

Harrison, C. (2008). Implacably hostile or appropriately protective? Women managing child contact in the context of domestic violence. *Violence Against Women*, 14, 381-405.

Lupri, E. (1990). Male violence in the home. In C. McKie & K. Thompson (Ed.), *Canadian Social Trends* (pp. 170-172). Toronto: Thompson Educational Publishing.

Radford, L., Hester, M., Humphries, J. & Woodfield, K.-S. (1997). For the sake of the children: The law, domestic violence, and child contact in England. *Women's Studies International Forum*, 20, 471-482.

Statistics Canada (2001). *Family Violence in Canada: A Statistical Profile*. Statistics Canada.

Watson, L.B., & Ancis, J.R. (2013). Power and control in the legal system: From marriage/ relationship to divorce and custody. *Violence Against Women*, 19(2), 166-186.

Van Horn, P., & McAlister Groves, B. (2006). Children exposed to domestic violence: Making trauma-informed custody and visitation decisions. *Juvenile and Family Court Journal*, 57(1), 51-60.

Domestic Violence: Is it Time to Leave?

Leaving an abusive relationship is hard. What may sound simple to an outsider is more complex to those on the inside. It's not as simple as it sounds.

Domestic violence (DV) involves a relationship in which there is criminal behavior. It's usually the man assaulting the woman, but not always. That is a very particular dynamic that affects everything in the family. It affects the parents, it affects the children, and it affects how your separation and divorce case works. If you are living within this difficult circumstance, then the stakes of your divorce are that much higher, and the need for a support system to help you through is much more urgent.

If you choose to leave the relationship and wish to break the cycle of domestic violence (DV) that you are living, you may want to consider a 2-step process.

1. Leave with a well thought out plan.
2. Break the Cycle and transition to a healthy new start.

This will put you on a measured path to begin your healing, while leaving safely. Note: please ensure you seek the appropriate professional help and advice to help ensure success, and leave safely.

Step 1. Leave with a well thought out plan

This is not the time to feel better or settle scores. Realize that you may be feeling a lot of stress right now, it's a situation that may have become all too familiar. When you leave, you may feel even more stressed and disoriented. Furthermore, you may feel out of control for a while, as you seek to put your life on track and begin to live on your own terms.

> Realize that you may be feeling a lot of stress right now, it's a situation that may have become all too familiar

This is the time to make your exit plan and put it into action. Feeling better happens later and does not involve your external family or the abusive partner. More information is provided below under Safe Living Training.

Develop a support network

Your support network provides stability, strength, and resources to help you through this tough time. This could be in the form of a domestic violence organization, a church, synagogue or other religious support group, a healthy family, and/or trusted friends. They should not provide you with advice, direction, or solutions.

Seek guidance and advice

This will come from an attorney, and possibly a competent Security Professional.

You and your children may need counseling. A therapist with a strong background and expertise in family and domestic violence situations would most likely be the counselor best for your situation right now. If you haven't already done so, seek out a qualified therapist now. The reason for this is simple. A good therapist will help you understand the issues, and what you may need to do. If you feel in danger or in an unsafe environment, don't doubt yourself, or your need to leave. Do not begin counseling until after you leave. Tell the therapist you are planning to leave and you will begin seeing them once you are in a safe setting. In the meantime, the therapist may be able to help you work on your safety plan.

Building your plan to leave.

Have you ever tried to "fix" a situation with very good intentions, but you actually make it much worse? This often happens when involving the Police in violent relationships. The Police may not be able to "Protect and Serve." They "Respond and Investigate." They may not always act in your best interests; they act in the interests of "the people" and the law. The police force does not always have the manpower or the budget to protect you. If you are in dire straits where you need protection, you should find a security professional that specializes in protection. However, don't hesitate to call the police if you feel your life, or your children are in danger.

When developing your plan to leave, you may want to consult with an attorney, security professional, and a DV organization about setting up an appointment with a detective. Choose these individuals carefully and ensure you're comfortable with them, as they will become your team. This is the time that you may want to file a report about the history of the relationship which will include: dates of abuses, hospital visits, social worker contacts, drug use, and any other evidence which you feel is relevant and important; your report should be detailed report and will contribute to building your case. If you haven't moved out yet, and abuse continues, document it with any evidence you have. Keep this report up to date.

Sustainability and Support

How will you support your family for the next year? You'll need safe places to live, food, counseling, transportation, legal costs, lots of changes. What if you need to quit your job? A lack of adequate resources is often a trigger to go back to the relationship. Plan for everything that could go wrong. This is the time to talk to your attorney about financial outcomes and interim support, in terms of spousal and child support. Your attorney can best advise you as to your rights and entitlements.

Cut off Direct Communication

Delegate communication to someone you trust and is in "good standing" with your partner, who has been abusive. This could be someone your partner feels he or she needs to be respectful to, such as your clergy or other person you hold in high regard. This delegate should:

- Have control of their emotions at all times and be completely trustworthy
- Be willing to spend lots of time communicating with both of you and your team
- Understand they are not entitled to an opinion
- Be a clear communicator, not only during speaking, but able to articulate demeanor, body language, and true intent to your team

In order to help ensure your abuser does not find you, consider a new phone number and new accounts for social media and email. Only interact with your team. You can pick up with old friends once the situation is safe and stable.

> You and your children may need counseling. A therapist with a strong background and expertise in family and domestic violence situations would most likely be the counselor best for your situation right now.

Leave your old phone number and accounts open and monitored by your attorney, communicator, and security professional.

Legal considerations

Cover your legal basis. Make sure you're not "kidnapping" your kids. If a court brings your actions or motives into question, you have your team: an attorney, a DV organization, and a detective to testify, which are very compelling in court.

In most instances, Courts will want to grant visitation rights to a parent – which may either be supervised access or not.

Prepare for this to happen. If it is not safe to let your children visit your co-parent, you must prepare a case before hand. Work with your attorney to develop your action plan prior to leaving so you know how best to proceed. Given that this is an emotionally stressful time, you want to ensure that you have emotional support so that you can better manage the legal side of divorce, and make informed decisions with confidence.

Begin your departure
Leaving is done for safety and a new start, not as retaliation.
Leave in a way that has the least impact on your abusive partner. You do not want unnecessary rage or embarrassment to fuel a response.

> Don't put yourself in that box and surround yourself with negativity and hopelessness. Constantly move toward positive goals.

If you can, finalize your plan at least a week in advance. This way, your team can have everything ready in advance, and can spot problems or overlooked items with time to fix them, or delay the evacuation.

On the day you leave, keep to the same schedule and routine so as not to bring attention to your plans. You may want to let your partner leave for work, and be gone for 1-2 hours to ensure no change in their schedule. Then, quickly pack the pre-determined items such as clothing, and some toys for your children. Ideally, your personal items should be light and easily transportable by two people; this may not be your last move.

Leaving without a trace
- Identify a communicator to speak with your spouse
- Use a vehicle and people that no one in your neighborhood will recognize.
- The pick up should happen fast; less than 15 minutes at your home.
- Turn off your phone, computer, and so on; begin your plan without looking back.

When your abusive partner returns home, your communicator

should call him/her and break the news in a well-scripted, calm manner. Do not let them return to an empty house and wonder where everyone is.

While this may seem oversimplified, the actual evacuation should be very efficient.

Step 2. Break the DV cycle and transition to a healthy new start

Seek counseling

Now that you've left and are on your plan, you need help for yourself and the kids. Check in with your counselor. Let them know you've left and need to begin sessions.

Support groups are for venting your anger and frustrations in a constructive manner and for learning from other's mistakes. They should not provide you with advice, direction, or solutions. You have an attorney, counselor, and security professional for that.

Caution: Only attend support groups that are well moderated by professionals and are kept on topic. Do not attend groups that are emotionally driven, they are counter-productive. Also, you do not need to make a group of friends who are victims. Don't put yourself in that box and surround yourself with negativity and hopelessness. Constantly move toward positive goals.

Safe Living Training

Many victims of violence are ruled by fear. How can you keep this from happening again? How can you trust again? How can you deal with the constant change that is happening in the first couple months after you leave?

This is where your security professional can really help, by conducting a Risk Assessment. Your security professional should work with you very closely in the first couple months after you leave. Their role is to:
- monitor the reaction of your spouse, court proceedings, and ensure you are safe during your normal routine.

- provide advice based on what is happening and proactively preparing you for what is, or could be coming up.
- help you to think through your goals upon separation or divorce. These conversations are great to have at the same time you are attending counseling. You can gain great insight from getting two points of view on the same topic.

Do a realistic assessment of the things that make you worry.

- Point out what elements you can control. Create a strategy to control them to the best of your ability. It is this element where solid advice and practical training will be an enormous help.
- Recognize the elements that you cannot control, but can prepare for. Make the appropriate arrangements and tailor them into your strategy. Once you know that you are controlling those elements as effectively as possible, the worry will begin to subside.
- Recognize the elements that are completely outside of your control. Accept them as such and be vigilant. Control the situations you allow yourself to be placed in; mitigating the elements outside of your control.

Vigilance and freedom from worry are the result of preparation. Similar to soldiers who train on how to handle horrible situations, they still feel fear, which causes them to maintain a higher degree of situational awareness. Rest assured, with your team, you can get through this to develop a successful and fulfilling life post separation and divorce.

Information and guidance provided by Tim Wenzel.
You may contact Tim by email at tim@wenzelgroup.net

Tim Wenzel is a Certified Protection Specialist and a Paramedic. He designs responsible security solutions that fit unique situations. He provides services to Global Business Leaders, Diplomats, and Government Agencies. Tim has a passion for assisting victims of Domestic Violence. He advocates using a comprehensive risk management strategy to ensure a safe transition for victims of violence.

Divorcing with Post Traumatic Stress: Getting the Help You Need

On a scale of stressful life events, divorce ranks second only to the death of a spouse or child. No doubt, divorce can be emotionally and financially devastating. One of the most serious health issues that can result from stress of divorce is depression. When you couple the emotional impact of divorce with Post Traumatic Stress Disorder (PTS), the impact and the outcomes can be much more complicated and serious – and at the extreme personal harm. The emotional toll of divorce can definitely ignite and worsen PTS symptoms. If you have been diagnosed with PTS, now is the time to ensure you get the help and support you need. It's important to treat the disorder before more symptoms and trouble occur. If your spouse is the one with PTS, you might seek help for yourself to better understand the issues and symptoms so as not to ignite any further emotional damage, and protect yourself from potential harm.

Post Traumatic Stress (PTS) is the development of emotional symptoms following exposure to a traumatic event and can occur as a result of a number of situations. Often time it is associated with combat situations, but can also result from violent crimes or from prolonged exposure to stressful events that

[1]. United States Department of Veteran Affairs

cause extreme emotional distress – such as divorce. PTS is categorized as an anxiety disorder. When an individual is confronted with situations that are triggers, this can further activate the problem.

The psychological impact of divorce on an individual with PTS is tremendous. Divorce is emotional, and when the emotions are ramped up and become extremely stressful, it can activate symptoms. The negative effects on a relationship of those experiencing PTS often triggers diminished parenting, aggression (both physical and verbal), domestic violence and substance abuse.

Coping through Post Traumatic Stress

Facts to be aware of if you are the one affected by PTS:
- For PTS to be considered a clinical condition it has to affect the individual's ability to function in the real world occupationally, socially, and/or legally beyond a thirty-day time period on a consistent basis.
- The condition tends to wax and wane over time activated by other stressors in life.
- Even though the stress you have now is unreasonable, the inciting experiences are real. Ensure that you talk to someone who can explain to you about your experience.
- Individuals who suffer from PTS are characteristically hostile or dangerous.

Treatment Options to Consider
- Seek the help of a mental health professional who has expertise in PTS
- Allow yourself time to heal and mourn the losses you experienced
- Talk to a trusted friend of counselor to discuss your experience and reflection
- Join a PTS support group
- Avoid alcohol and drugs
- Develop healthy habits, and focus on relaxation techniques, getting ample sleep and eating healthfully

Divorce can aggravate how an individual copes through PTS. As a result, it is critical to get the appropriate assistance as soon as you feel your symptoms are worsening and you feel in "crisis" mode. Some of the symptoms to be aware of include:

- Perceived Threats (Verbal/Physical)
- Perceived Misuse of Power
- Perceived Conflict
- Loud Noises
- Particular Smells
- Fast/Hidden Movements
- Crowds/Confusion
- Alcohol/Drug Usage
- Loss of a Relationship (divorce, break up), job loss, grieving a loved one
- Accumulative Trauma
- Anger, Rage, destructive behavior
- Experiencing War or Trauma Triggers (Cues)
- Vivid Flashbacks, disturbing Nightmares
- Emotional Detachment/Feeling Loss
- Hyper-Vigilance/Hyper-Arousal
- Alcohol/Substance Abuse
- Medical Problems/Pain

The divorce process may trigger:
- Avoidance of things that remind the individual of the event
- Increased stimulation resulting in a fight or flight response such as:
- Physical reactions to stress, including: an increase in heart rate, narrowing of vision, muscle tension, sweating, and more sensitive hearing.
- Adaptive changes preparing you for immediate action to fight, flee, or freeze
- Triggers can lead to dissociation (a break from reality) through flashbacks.

- Hyper-vigilance, anger outbursts, startle response
- Re-experiencing the event through hallucinations, dissociative flashbacks, emotional numbing
- Increased or start of substance abuse
- Talk of self harm

Divorce could heighten the self-harm factor, now is not the time to wait to see if you'll feel better. The emotional aspects to divorce might leave you feeling raw, bitter and angry. If you are feeling this intense emotional pain, then it is important that you see a skilled therapist to help you through this difficult time.

Other considerations:
- Speak with friends who share your PTS related experiences. Because they were there, their points and perspectives are very valid and may help you see that some of your thoughts or fears may be unreasonable or exaggerated.

- Some individuals distrust their counselor or therapist, and this is sometimes associated with posttraumatic stress. If this is your experience, bring a friend to your therapy appointment who understands what you've been going through, but not themselves suffering from PTS. This may help validate what the counselor says, or communicate what the patient is experiencing by providing context. Obviously the friend must be onboard with the counselor's treatment plan to help stay the course.

- If you are attending a group therapy session with PTS groups, ensure that they are well moderated so as not to become an unhealthy and enabling environment.

> While it may be difficult for you to understand the depression and anxiety your spouse is experiencing, it is important to be compassionate and understanding, especially now as emotions are heightened due to divorce.

Understanding and Considerations When Post Traumatic Stress is Ignited

While it may be difficult for you to understand the depression and anxiety your spouse is experiencing, it is important to be compassionate and understanding, especially now as emotions are heightened due to divorce. However, it is necessary for everyone's well being to take proper precautions if you feel threatened. You may want to consider developing an action plan should you feel threatened in any way.

> Divorce can take a huge emotional toll on the family. While emotions are at an all time high, and feelings are at an all time low, it is important to find professionals who understand both sides of the experience.

Developing Your Safety Plan

- Identify a "safe house" location which you can easily access, and keep the an emergency kit handy including:
    - a change of clothes for you and your children
    - necessities and toiletries
    - list of important phone numbers
    - emergency funds
    - a photocopy of your identification such as driver's license, credit cards and so on
    - emergency cell phone with a pay as you go card
- In extreme cases, call the police
- Call your lawyer immediately, if you have retained legal counsel.

Divorcing with Post Traumatic Stress

Divorce can take a huge emotional toll on the family. While emotions are at an all time high, and feelings are at an all time low, it is important to find professionals (family law lawyers, social workers, psychiatrists, and parenting experts) who understand both sides of the experience – from the individual with PTS, to the individual married to someone with PTS. The last thing you want to do is aggravate the issues and ignite the negative behaviors associated with PTS.

Factors to consider:
- Expressing emotions and feelings can be difficult for someone with PTS. When developing the Separation Agreement, this is an important aspect to discuss with your family law lawyer and other professionals.
- A safety measure clause included the parenting plan, for example supervised access for the parent with PTS.
- A restraining order/protective order
- How safe are you with a protective order
- Other safety options to discuss with your lawyer.

Putting your children's best interest first

In the most amicable of circumstances divorce can be a painful experience for children, but over time, and when parents co-parent effectively, kids can adapt and adjust and are no different than kids from intact families. However, when a parent has PTS, the impact is can be confusing and devastating. Children may not understand what is happening or why. They may worry about their parent or worry that the parent cannot take care of them. The following is a list of how a parent's PTS symptoms might affect his or her children[1].

- Because re-experience of symptoms is so upsetting, people with PTS try not to think about the event. If you have PTS, you may want to try avoiding places and things that remind you of the trauma. Or you may not feel like doing things that used to be fun, like going to the movies or your child's event. It can also be hard for people with PTS to have good feelings. You may feel "cut off" from family and children. As a result, children may feel that the parent with PTS does not care about them.
- People with PTS tend to be anxious and "on edge." With PTS, you might have trouble sleeping or paying attention. You might be grouchy or angry much of the time. You may be easily scared, or overly worried about your safety or the safety of your loved ones. It is easy to see how these problems can affect family members. For example, acting grumpy can make a parent seem mean or angry. Since they do not understand the symptoms of PTS, children may wonder whether their parent loves them.

- A parent's PTS symptoms are directly linked to their child's responses. Children usually respond in a number of ways, for example:
    - A child might feel and behave just like their parent as a way of trying to connect with the parent. The child might show some of the same symptoms as the parent with PTS.
    - A child may take on the adult role to fill in for the parent with PTS; acting too grown-up for his/ her age.
    - Some children do not get help with their feelings. This can lead to problems at school, sadness, and relationship problems later in life.
    - At times it may be very difficult for therapists to help children caught in a difficult divorce situation. Children are in survival mode and develop ways of coping by either avoiding talking to adults, or trying to please all adults involved in turn. Sometimes it is best for parents to get some coaching from a child therapist to help the children themselves, and maintain the children's trust in the middle of the turmoil.
- Some research shows that children of veterans with PTS are more likely to have problems with behaviors and school and problems getting along with others. Their parents see them as more sad, anxious, aggressive, and hyper than children of someone who does not have PTS. Some research has also found that PTS in a parent is related to violence in the home and to children acting violent.
- Some children and teenagers of individuals with PTS are more sad and anxious than their peers. The impact of a parent's PTS symptoms on a child is sometimes called "secondary traumatization." Since violence occurs in some homes in which a parent has PTS, the children may also develop their own PTS symptoms related to the violence. A child's PTS symptoms can get worse if there is not a parent who can help the child feel better.

Can children get Post Traumatic Stress from their parents?

In some rare instances, it is possible for children to show signs of PTS because they are upset by their parent's symptoms. For example, a child may have nightmares about the parent's trauma, or a child might have trouble paying attention at school because she is thinking about her parent's problems. Trauma symptoms can also be passed from parent to child or between generations. This is called "intergenerational transmission of trauma." Here is how it happens:

- When a family silences a child, or teaches him to not talk about disturbing events, thoughts, or feelings, the child's anxiety gets worse. He may start to worry about causing the parent's symptoms if he talks about the trauma. He may create his own ideas about what happened to the parent, which can be worse than what actually happened.
- Sometimes parents share too many full details about the events. Children then can start to experience their own set of PTS symptoms in response to these terrible images.
- A child may begin to share in her parent's symptoms as a way to connect with the parent, or because this behavior seems normal in the home environment.
- Children may also repeat or re-do some aspect of the trauma because they see that their parent has difficulty separating the past trauma from the present moment.

Other considerations:
- Talk to your children about the impending divorce, and explain about their parent's behavior and difficulties. You might even speak to a counselor or therapist with advice on how to manage the conversation.
- Try to anticipate your children's questions and reactions, and be prepared to respond.
- Encourage your children to talk about their feelings.
- If your child is having troubling coping, seek the help of a qualified therapist with expertise in PTS to assist your child in understanding this condition, and understand that their parent's symptoms are not their fault. Parents need to keep the issue of trust with the therapist foremost in their mind.
- Develop a parenting plan that accommodates the emotional aspects and reactions of PTS.
- Work with your co-parent and a professional to help the children understand their parent's mental health, and what to do in a danger-

ous situation

- Get help and treatment if you find it difficult to maintain a healthy relationship with your children

It's important to be aware that trauma disturbs our normal life beliefs and turns our world upside down, causing confusion, disbelief, feelings of vulnerability, a loss of meaning and purpose in life. It changes our self-image or self-esteem. The family system is in complete flux, and what affects one person may impact everyone in the family.

SEPARATING SAFELY

Knowing the risks of abuse following separation and divorce for you and your children.

Are you at risk?

Research demonstrates that the risk of lethal violence is particularly high in the first few months following separation (Campbell, Glass, Sharps, Laughon, & Bloom, 2007). In addition to an elevated risk of lethal violence, there is also an increased risk for non-lethal violence post-separation. Evidence suggests that those who are physically violent against their partner before a separation will often become psychologically violent following separation (Brownridge, 2006). Thirty percent of divorced or separated men had perpetrated acts of violence against their partners in a national sample of 1834 Canadians, in comparison to only eighteen percent of their married counterparts (Lupri, 1990).

What about with your children?

Following divorce, violent partners have been shown to use access with children or legal custody proceedings to control their former partners (Radford et al., 1997; Harrison, 2008).

Watson and Ancis (2013) found that in couples where abuse was a factor in their married or former relationship, during divorce proceedings, child support litigation, custody and visitation battles, and prolonging the case were used against abuse victims as a way for perpetrators to exert power and control over their former spouses even in divorce. This control is not only exerted over the parent, but also the children, as the abusive parent often threaten to take the children away or use the children as weapons against the other parent by undermining the non-abusive parent's credibility and telling the children the separation is their fault (Van Horn & McAlister Groves, 2006).

Are you being abusive?

If you are abusing your former partner, you first need to accept that you have a problem that requires help. No form of abuse is acceptable, and while some may seem more serious than others, they can escalate and all need to be addressed. Once you have accepted that there is a problem, you have already become part of the solution. You need to know that help is available to you, the

---

Partner Assault Response (PAR) programs, a component of Ontario's Domestic Violence Court program, are specialized counselling and educational services offered by community-based agencies to people who have assaulted their partners.

While an offender is in the PAR program, staff offer their partner help with safety planning, referrals to community resources, and information about the offender's progress. To find the PAR office nearest you, call the Victim Support Line toll-free at 1-888-579-2888, or 416-314-2447 in the Greater Toronto Area.

following agencies will direct you to the best place to get it.

What do I do?

To prevent yourself from continuing this process and placing yourself and your family at risk, you should:

- Exchange the children in a *public place* - if this is impossible, exchange the children outside the home (i.e., on the sidewalk, for instance)
- *Shorten the time* it takes to hand over the children by making sure everything is ready when your former partner is scheduled to pick them up
- *Minimize communication* with your former partner as much as possible. You can do this by, writing any necessary information regarding the children in a diary kept in one of the children's bag, communicating via e-mail rather than phone.
- *Seek help* by consulting with a mental health professional or agency that will support you in working on healthier ways to cope with your separation or divorce
- *Take some time* to cool down when you become upset with your former partner, find a healthy way to deal with it (i.e., go for a walk, exercise, talk to a friend, etc.)
- *Be more aware* of how what you say and do may be perceived by your former partner and children and try to correct it before it is understood negatively
- Harass your former partner by legal means - for instance, making false allegations about your former partner to child protective services or filing repeated family law claims

Psychological

Do you…

- Makes your former partner feel guilty and inadequate with the things you say
- Criticizes what your former partner does and how they do it
- Threatens to kidnap your children if your former partner does not comply with what you want
- Threaten to take custody away from your former partner or prevent them from obtaining custody

- Threaten to harm your former partner physically
- Make suicide threats
- Threatens to kill your former partner or your children

Bryanne Harris, M.A. (Counselling Psychology). You may contact Ms. Harris by e-mail atbharri33@uwo.ca

Bryanne Harris is a Psychologist (Cand. Reg.) specializing in high-conflict divorce and court-ordered assessments. She recently received her Master of Arts in Counselling Psychology from the University of Western Ontario in London, Ontario and completed her Master's Thesis on gender bias in parental alienation in the Canadian court system. Ms. Harris has also conducted research on domestic violence, divorce, and teacher sexual misconduct, among other topics.

Resources

Brownridge, D.A. (2006). Violence against women post-separation. *Aggression and Violent Behavior*, 11, 514-530.

Campbell, J.C., Glass, N., Sharps, P.W., Laughon, K., & Bloom, T. (2007). Intimate partner homicide: Review and implications of research and policy. *Trauma, Violence & Abuse*, 8, 246-269.

Harrison, C. (2008). Implacably hostile or appropriately protective? Women managing child contact in the context of domestic violence. *Violence Against Women*, 14, 381-405.

Lupri, E. (1990). Male violence in the home. In C. McKie & K. Thompson (Ed.), *Canadian Social Trends* (pp. 170-172). Toronto: Thompson Educational Publishing.

Radford, L., Hester, M., Humphries, J. & Woodfield, K.-S. (1997). For the sake of the children: The law, domestic violence, and child contact in England. *Women's Studies International Forum*, 20, 471-482.

Statistics Canada (2001). *Family Violence in Canada: A Statistical Profile*. Statistics Canada.

Watson, L.B., & Ancis, J.R. (2013). Power and control in the legal system: From marriage/ relationship to divorce and custody. *Violence Against Women*, 19(2), 166-186.

Van Horn, P., & McAlister Groves, B. (2006). Children exposed to domestic violence: Making trauma-informed custody and visitation decisions. *Juvenile and Family Court Journal*, 57(1), 51-60.

About the Author

Deborah Moskovitch is a Divorce Coach supporting people in having more positive outcomes from their divorce, for a happier and healthier future. She understands divorce, because she has been through her own seven-year struggle that ended more than 10 years ago. That process inspired Deborah to hunt for less painful ways to manage the divorce process and share it with others. Since then, she has researched and shared proven strategies and advice from 100 of North American's top divorce lawyers, financial advisors, counselors and other experts in her best selling resource book, The Smart Divorce, now in its third printing.

Responding to the demand for "neutral" support, Deborah founded, The Smart Divorce® to provide informative resources, support coaching and powerful educational tools to empower and free people during this difficult time. As a Divorce Coach, she provides private one-on-one coaching, events, and other unique divorce support services for individuals and for organizations across North America. The Smart Divorce® is your one stop shop for cost effective divorce support. She's in your camp!

Deborah's goal is always to help you get through your divorce smarter with your family, your finances and your sanity intact, while saving you time and money. She remains curious and questioning, as an online radio host, of the informative Radio Show, The Smart Divorce on Divorce Source Radio and as a regular columnist for the Huffington Post and More Magazine. In addition, she is a public speaker and media contact on the topic of divorce how-to. She has been interviewed on more that 40 television and radio shows, and is widely quoted in Canadian and U.S. print and online publications.

Deborah holds degrees in economics and business administration from Toronto's York University. As an advocate for giving back, she is active in her local Canadian and United States communities where she is:

- On the Ontario board of directors of the Association of

Family and Conciliation Courts (AFCC) (2008 – 2013), an international association of professionals dedicated to improving the lives of children and families through the resolution of family conflict; and a recipient of the AFCC-O 2012 Distinguished Service Award.

- On the virtual workgroup of the Honoring Families Initiative of IAALS, dedicated to empirically informed models to ensure greater accessibility, efficiency, and fairness in divorce and child custody matters.
- On the advisory panel/Divorce Team for Women Moving On in Florida.
- On the editorial advisory board and columnist for NEXT magazine.
- A founding board member of the Neuro Family Law Institute, created with a vision of transforming family law into a more posi---tive experience for separating families.

Contributors

I am indebted to the contributors of The Smart Divorce Smart Guide who have provided their smart tips and knowledge to help me, help you, save time, money – and your sanity

Nathalie Boutet – Lawyer, Boutet Family Law
http://www.boutetfamilylaw.com
nboutet@boutetfamilylaw.com
Legal Separation – The Power of Setting Proper Expectations

Bill Eddy, LCSW, Esq.
http://www.highconflictinstitute.com
info@highconflictinstitute.com
What to Tell the Kids About a High-Conflict Co-Parent
A B.I.F.F. Response to Hostile Email

Bryanne Harris, M.A. (Counselling Psychology)
bharri33@uwo.ca
Separating Safely: Knowing the Risks of Abuse
Separating Safely: Are You Abusive?

Jeffery Landers, CDFA – Divorce Financial Strategist™ and the founder of Bedrock Divorce Advisors
http://www.BedrockDivorce.com
landers@bedrockdivorce.com
Understanding How Assets Get Divided in Divorce
Financial Information Checklist - The Important Financial Steps Required to Prepare for Divorce

Mark Rye, Ph. D. – Clinical psychologist and Associate Professor of Psychology at Skidmore College, and the Skidmore College Positive Psychology Research team.
mrye@skidmore.edu
A Journey Toward Forgiveness Following Divorce

Phil Stahl, Ph.D.
http://parentingafterdivorce.com/
philipstahlphd@gmail.com
Cooperative Parenting or Parallel Parenting

Jacqueline Vanbetlehem, RSW, Acc.F.M.
http://www.vanbetlehem.ca
jacqueline@vanbetlehem.ca
How to Tell Your Spouse You Want a Divorce

Mike Webster, Ed.D., R. Psych
conman@uniserve.com
How to Increase Your Ability to Cope When Divorcing

Tim Wenzel
http://www.wenzelgroup.net
tim@wenzelgroup.net
Domestic Violence: Is it Time to Leave?

Books

Eddy, Bill LCSW, Esq. and Saposnek, Donald T., Ph.D. SPLITTING AMERICA: *How Politicians, Super PACs and the News Media Mirror High Conflict Divorce*

Eddy, Bill LCSW, Esq. *The Future of Family Court: Structure, Skills and Less Stress*

Eddy, Bill LCSW, Esq. and Kreger, Randi. *Splitting: Protecting Yourself While Divorcing Someone a Borderline or Narcissistic Personality Disorder*

Eddy, Bill LCSW, Esq. *BIFF: Quick Responses to High Conflict People, Their Personal Attacks, Hostile Email and Social Media Meltdowns*

Eddy, Bill LCSW, Esq. *Don't Alienate The Kids! Raising Resilient Children While Avoiding High Conflict Divorce*

Moskovitch, Deborah. *The Smart Divorce: Proven Strategies and Valuable Advice from 100 Top Divorce Lawyers, Financial Advisers, Counselor, and Other Experts.* Chicago: Chicago Review Press, 2007.

Stahl, Philip M., Ph.D. *Complex Issues in Child Custody Evaluations.* California: Sage Publications, Inc, 1999.

Stahl, Philip M., Ph.D. *Parenting After Divorce: A Guide to Resolving Conflicts and Meeting Your Children's Needs.* California: Impact Publishers, 2000.

Listed below are some books that might be helpful if you are interested in reading more about forgiveness; as suggested by Dr. Mark Rye.

Luskin, Fred. Forgive for Good

Worthington, Everett. Five Steps to Forgiveness: The Art and Science of Forgiving

Enright, Robert D. Forgiveness Is a Choice: A Step-By-Step Process for Resolving Anger and Restoring Hope

Kendall, R.T. How to Forgive Ourselves Totally: Begin Again by Breaking Free From Past Mistakes

References

References for A Journey Toward Forgiveness Following Divorce, by Mark Rye, Ph.D. and the Skidmore College Positive Psychology Research team.

Bonach, K. (2009). Empirical support for the application of the forgiveness intervention model to postdivorce coparenting. *Journal of Divorce & Remarriage*, 50(1), 38-54. doi:10.1080/10502550802365631

Bonach, K., & Sales, E. (2002). Forgiveness as a mediator between post divorce cognitive processes and coparenting quality. *Journal of Divorce & Remarriage*, 38(1-2), 17-38. doi:10.1300/J087v38n01_02

Enright, R.D. (2001). *Forgiveness is a choice: A step-by-step process for resolving anger and restoring hope*. Washington, DC: American Psychology Association.

Fincham, F. D., Jackson, H., & Beach, S. R. H. (2005). Transgression severity and forgiveness: Different moderators for objective and subjective severity. *Journal of Social and Clinical Psychology*, 24(6), 860-875. doi:10.1521/jscp.2005.24.6.860

Freedman, S. R., & Enright, R. D. (1996). Forgiveness as an intervention goal with incest survivors. *Journal of Consulting and Clinical Psychology*, 64(5), 983-992. doi:10.1037/0022-006X.64.5.983

Kendall, R.T. (2007). *How to forgive ourselves totally: Begin again by breaking free from past mistakes*. Lake Mary, FL: Charisma House.

Luskin, F. (2003). *Forgive for good*. New York, NY: HarperOne.

Nabi, H., Singh-Manoux, A., Ferrie, J. E., Marmot, M. G., Melchior, M., & Kivimäki, M. (2010). Hospitality and depressive mood: Results from the whitehall II prospective cohort study. *Psychological Medicine: A*

Journal of Research in Psychiatry and the Allied Sciences, 40(3), 405-413. doi:10.1017/S0033291709990432

Ohbuchi, K., Kameda, M., & Agarie, N. (1989). Apology as aggression control: Its role in mediating appraisal of and response to harm. *Journal of Personality and Social Psychology*, 56(2), 219-227. doi:10.1037/0022-3514.56.2.219

Rohde-Brown, J., & Rudestam, K. E. (2011). The role of forgiveness in divorce adjustment and the impact of affect. *Journal of Divorce & Remarriage*, 52(2), 109-124. doi:10.1080/10502556.2011.546233

Rye, M. S., Folck, C. D., Heim, T. A., Olszewski, B. T., & Traina, E. (2004). Forgiveness of an ex-spouse: How does it relate to mental health following a divorce? *Journal of Divorce & Remarriage*, 41(3-4), 31-51. doi:10.1300/J087v41n03_02

Trinder, L., Kellet, J., & Swift, L. (2008). The relationship between contact and child adjustment in high conflict cases after divorce or separation. *Child and Adolescent Mental Health*, 13(4), 181-187. doi:10.1111/j.1475-3588.2008.00484.x

Vandervoort, D. J. (2006). Hostility and health: Mediating effects of belief systems and coping styles. *Current Psychology: A Journal for Diverse Perspectives on Diverse Psychological* Issues, 25(1), 50-66. doi:10.1007/s12144-006-1016-2

Witvliet, C. V. (2001). Forgiveness and health: Review and reflections on a matter of faith, feelings, and physiology. *Journal of Psychology and Theology*, 29(3), 212-224.

Wade, N. G., & Worthington, E. L. J. (2005). In search of a common core: A content analysis of interventions to promote forgiveness. *Psychotherapy: Theory, Research, Practice, Training*, 42(2), 160-177. doi:10.1037/0033-3204.42.2.160

Wohl, M. J. A., DeShea, L., & Wahkinney, R. L. (2008). Looking within: Measuring state self-forgiveness and its relationship to psychological well-being. *Canadian Journal of Behavioural Science/Revue Canadienne Des Sciences Du Comportement*, 40(1), 1-10. doi:10.1037/0008-400x.40.1.1.1

Worthington, E. L. (1998). An empathy-humility-commitment model of forgiveness applied within family dyads. *Journal of Family Therapy*, 20(1), 59-76. doi:10.1111/1467-6427.00068

Worthington, E.L. (2001). *Five steps to forgiveness: The art and science of forgiving.* New York, NY: Crown.

Notes

Notes

Notes

www.ingramcontent.com/pod-product-compliance
Lightning Source LLC
Chambersburg PA
CBHW070453090426
42735CB00012B/2538